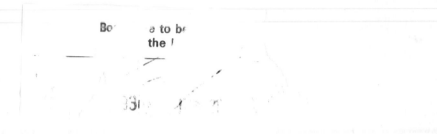

Bo   e to be
        the

2 7 OCT 1999

Profitable Practice Management

Other titles from E & FN Spon

Architectural Management
M.P. Nicholson

Building Economics
Theory and Practice
R.T. Ruegg and H.E. Marshall

Introduction to Building
Procurement Systems
J.W.E. Masterman

Construction Conflicts
Management and Resolution
P. Fenn and R. Gameson

Construction Contracts
Law and management
J.R. Murdoch and W. Hughes

A Concise Introduction to
Engineering Economics
P. Cassimatis

The Idea of Building
S. Groák

Investment, Procurement and
Performance in Construction
P. Venmore-Rowland, P. Brandon and
T. Mole

The Management of Quality in
Construction
J.L. Ashford

Management, Quality and
Economics in Building
P. Brandon and A. Bezelga

Practice Management
New perspectives for the
construction professional
P. Barrett and R. Males

Project Management Demystified

Today's tools and techniques
G. Reiss

Spon's Budget Estimating
Handbook
Spain and Partners

Spon's Construction Cost and Price
Indices Handbook
B.A. Tysoe and M.C. Fleming

Effective Speaking
Communicating in speech
C. Turk

Effective Writing
Improving scientific, technical and
business communication
2nd Edition
C. Turk and J. Kirkman

Good Style
Writing for science and technology
J. Kirkman

Writing Successfully in Science
M. O'Connor

Journals

Construction Management and
Economics
Editors: R. Bon and W. Hughes

Building Research and Information
Editor: A. Kirk

For more information on these and other titles please contact:
The Promotion Department, E & FN Spon, 2–6 Boundary Row, London,
SE1 8HN. Telephone 071–522–9966.

Profitable Practice Management

For the construction professional

Peter Barrett

Director of Policy Coordination
Department of Surveying
The University of Salford, UK

E & FN SPON

An Imprint of Chapman & Hall

London · Glasgow · New York · Tokyo · Melbourne · Madras

Published by E & FN Spon, an imprint of Chapman & Hall, 2–6 Boundary Row, London SE1 8HN

Chapman & Hall, 2–6 Boundary Row, London SE1 8HN, UK

Blackie Academic & Professional, Wester Cleddens Road, Bishopbriggs, Glasgow G64 2NZ, UK

Chapman & Hall Inc., 29 West 35th Street, New York NY10001, USA

Chapman & Hall Japan, Thomson Publishing Japan, Hirakawacho Nemoto Building, 6F, 1-7-11 Hirakawa-cho, Chiyoda-ku, Tokyo 102, Japan

Chapman & Hall Australia, Thomas Nelson Australia, 102 Dodds Street, South Melbourne, Victoria 3205, Australia

Chapman & Hall India, R. Seshadri, 32 Second Main Road, CIT East, Madras 600 035, India

First edition 1993

© 1993 Peter Barrett

Typeset in 10/12pt Times by ROM-Data Corp. Ltd., Falmouth, Cornwall
Printed in Great Britain by TJ Press Ltd., Padstow, Cornwall

ISBN 0 419 15590 2

A catalogue record for this book is available from the British Library

Library of Congress Cataloging-in-Publication data

Barrett, Peter.
    Profitable practice management / Peter Barret. – 1st ed.
        p.   cm.
    Includes bibliographical references and index.
    ISBN 0–419–15590–2
    1. Architectural practice–United States–Management.   I. Title.
NA1996. B37   1993
720'. 68–dc20   92–38837
                                                          CIP

∞ Printed on permanent acid-free text paper, manufactured in accordance with the proposed ANSI/NISO Z 39.48–199X and ANSI Z 39.48–1984

To Lucinda, Oliver, Camilla, Raphaella
and Clementine

CONTENTS

Acknowledgements

Chapter 10 was first published as a paper entitled 'The Synthesis of an Analytical Method for Professional Service Firms' in the *International Journal of Service Management*, volume 1, number 2, pp. 17–32, 1990.

Introduction

Managing the professional firm, or practice management, is obviously something that has been done for as long as there have been professional firms. It is arguable that, in the past, if your firm produced good-quality work, this would ensure a continued flow of commissions and all involved could enjoy a reasonable standard of living.

Over recent years many of the factors impinging on the construction professions have changed and as a result the need has become apparent for an emphasis on managing **the firm itself** as well as excelling at the projects done. This in turn demands critical analyses of alternative approaches and the development of hypotheses and models as guides to action.

So, how far has this process progressed and which are the forces at work?

0.1 BACKGROUND

0.1.1 Historically

Until relatively recently there has been little research into the management of the professional firm (Maister, 1982, p. 15; Grönroos, 1983, p. 17). Some early work was done by the RIBA, notably their major study of architectural firms, *The Architect and his Office* (RIBA, 1962). This, however, preceded significant advances in management research. To date the construction professions have been slow to draw from this source, but a wealth of ideas and advice exists which can, with care, be used.

In the past the need for rigorous analysis of how professional firms can best react to various contingencies was perhaps of little practical interest, but in the late 1970s Nisbet (1977) charted the declining fortunes of the professions within society since Victorian times. There have been much more profound changes since then.

0.1.2 Competition

A report commissioned by the Royal Institution of Chartered Surveyors (RICS) in 1985 states:

A combination of slowing market growth and deregulation, both in the markets served by surveyors and those served by other adjacent professionals (e.g. architects, accountants, solicitors), have combined to greatly increase competition and alter buyer behaviour. Many private surveying practices have consequently found themselves under increasing economic and competitive pressure. (MAC, 1985, p. 89)

Examples related to increased competition are the abolition of scale fees, due in large part to the influence of the Office of Fair Trading (Director General OFT, 1986), and the relaxation of professional codes of conduct to allow more explicit approaches to be made to prospective clients for work (e.g. RICS, 1988).

Alterations in 'buyer behaviour' are closely linked to the above, but a very topical example is the declared intention of some of the larger companies that, at some time in the future, they will only use consultants on the DTI's register of 'quality assured firms' (e.g. Dalton, 1987, pp. 360–6). A less defined but very real change is the increasing willingness of clients to resort to litigation if dissatisfied. This is evidenced by massive increases in the indemnity insurance premiums paid by firms over recent years. Increases of 100% and over were experienced in 1985 (Kindred and Moreton, 1988) and further, less severe, escalation has occurred since. These changes are put in perspective by Rueschemeyer's historical analysis (1983, pp. 45–8). He shows that there has always been a dynamic relationship between 'the professions' and the society within which they exist, centred on the extent to which the professions are allowed discretion to regulate their own manner of operating.

0.1.3 Technology

A further area of rapid change is technology, especially in the field of information technology. For example: computer power allows the analysis of massive quantities of data into information to support decisions; fax machines allow complex messages to be relayed over huge distances instantly; expert systems make more freely available knowledge sources hitherto highly inaccessible; and CAD systems make possible greater experimentation, and strikingly realistic illustration, in the design process.

The implications for practice management are manifold. Professional firms are knowledge-based and the delivery of this knowledge to the client is the essence of their service. Knowledge in transit is information. The above examples illustrate that technology enables information to be manipulated ever more flexibly in time, space and substance.

0.1.4 Education

In addition to the above factors, the professions themselves have made radical changes in terms of how individuals enter practice. Historically, people would join a firm from school and train part-time, graduating from office junior to junior assistant, and so on. This implicitly provided for a process of socialization during which traditional professional norms were inculcated in the aspiring professional (Bierhoff and Klein, 1988, pp. 256–7). As a result, the professions were homogenized to an extent and certainly they were subject to a strong integrating force.

Lately the predominant mode of qualifying has become the exempting degree. This approach results in new entrants to the professions beginning their working careers at much more senior levels and the opportunity for the socialization of a relatively unformed (professionally) individual is no longer available. Thus, those making up the workforce of the professions are likely to be much more diverse in what they consider to be acceptable and, indeed, possible.

Another factor that has changed is the rising emphasis given to management as a topic in the educational process. Qualified practitioners have also sought and supported an increasing number of continuing professional development seminars/courses on management-related topics. Thus, both before and after qualification, the construction professional is likely to have a greater familiarity with general management concepts and practices.

0.1.5 Business or practice?

It can be seen from the above that there have been great changes recently in the environment of the professional firm. As a result, the perceived importance of managing **the firm** effectively has increased considerably.

> Practice management is now a key skill, and it is through effective practice management that a firm can achieve a distinctive competitive position. (MAC, 1985, p. 90)

Therefore, the majority of firms are faced with a decision: do they continue as traditional practices or do they take on business attitudes and techniques? Coxe *et al.* (1987, p. 23) suggest a continuum from practice-centred business to business-centred practice. McGee (1985, pp. 21–2) makes a distinction between 'market' and 'professional' service firms.

Some work by McFadzean-Ferguson (1985, pp. 82–3) suggests that among civil engineering firms the conflict between 'their professional outlook and aspirations and the need for business success to support it' (p. 83) is causing tensions and resulting in some firms moving towards a more commercial mode of operation.

A practical corollary of this shift is the relaxation of the professional codes to allow firms to practice with limited liability (e.g. RICS, 1988). It is not unusual, now, to find that professionals are using the company structure.

0.2 SYNTHESIS

It is apparent that various forces are at work causing a profound change in the way that professional firms are managed. Kurt Lewin (1947) proposed the use of 'force

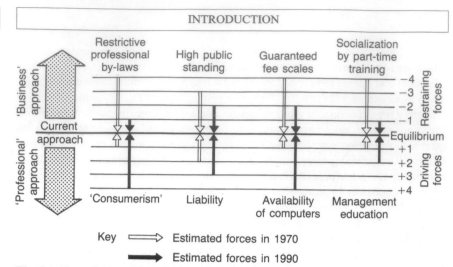

Key ⟹ Estimated forces in 1970
⟹ Estimated forces in 1990

Fig. 0.1 Force field analysis of approach to practice management

fields' in the analysis of 'quasi-stationary equilibria' which typify many social situations. In the case of the construction-related professions the driving forces and restraining forces salient to changes along the business/profession continuum might be as shown in Figure 0.1.

Changes over the last decade, and certainly over the last two, have seen the driving forces towards a business-oriented approach to practice management strengthen considerably, while restraining forces have, if anything, dwindled. Change seems inevitable. It cannot be ignored or avoided.

Garrett (1981, p. 838) neatly applies to professional firms Revan's suggestion that, to survive, an organism must learn at a faster rate than the rate of change it faces. If profound change is upon us then those managing professional firms must learn new skills, assimilate alternative perspectives and, above all, react by facing the challenges with an open mind that does not avoid the difficult questions but determines courses of action that build on strengths and eliminate weaknesses.

But, in which areas are these developments required?

0.3 FACETS OF PRACTICE MANAGEMENT

Managers of professional firms face multi-faceted problems of great diversity. A recent study (Barrett, 1990a) identified four main interactions (Table 0.1), includ-

Table 0.1 Aggregate time/effort expended

Interaction	%
Long-term planning	2
Managing the current clients/factors	8
Managing own staff	7
Fee-earning work	83

ing fee-earning work, which accounted for aggregate time/effort expended (by all staff), within the 21 professional firms studied.

Only one of the partners and directors interviewed concentrated solely on the first three categories shown in the table – that is, was a full-time manager of the firm. All the others operated part time, often with considerable project commitments. Thus, managers of professional firms are typically stretched in several directions, ranging from strategy formulation to the immediate demands of a project.

This is, of course, problematic in the turbulent environment already described. In stable conditions an amateur, part-time approach could suffice. In current circumstances the cycle of external changes, problems, decisions, internal changes and so on makes much greater demands on the manager both quantitatively (time) and qualitatively (knowledge and skills).

Based on the results of research into the factors leading to profitability in the construction-related professions (Barrett, 1989) it is essential to include 'soft' or 'people' factors as well as 'hard' task-focused factors if a full understanding of organizational performance is to be achieved. Thus, Part Two of this book focuses on managing the firm's **tasks**, but is complemented by Part Three which is concerned with managing the firm's **staff**.

The above sections of the book are preceded by consideration of the nature of profitability and research results on the major factors which influence it. More details of the research are given in Chapter 10 which, together with a chapter on a number of key issues for the future, makes up Part Four.

0.4 CONCLUSION

Profound changes have impacted on the professional firms involved in construction and this has created forces for change in the way such firms are managed. There will be a tendency for firms to be managed in a more proactive way in future, with reduced constraints and greater levels of risk.

It is highly desirable that the changes that take place do so against a background of relevant research which draws widely from adjacent fields of study, but remains firmly focused on the construction professions. Many underlying assumptions need to be questioned and examined objectively for relevance in the changed circumstances. Only through this painful process (Sidgewick, 1983) will the disruptive effects of the inevitable turbulence be reduced and the available opportunities be identified and grasped.

This book is offered as a contribution to the process of developing a corpus of management theory **for the construction professions**.

PART ONE

Overview

The main determinants of profit | 1

Before considering the determinants of profit it is first necessary to look more closely at profitability as a performance measure.

1.1 WHAT IS PROFIT?

1.1.1 Profit as an objective

Firms in private practice are generally assumed to be in existence primarily to generate a profit for the owners, usually the partners. In economic theory the objective of a firm is to maximize profit. These are very simplistic views of profit and there may be many other reasons why people are in practice. For instance:

- they may enjoy designing buildings, etc, *per se*;
- they may want to have a beneficial influence on the development of the environment;
- they may like working with the other people in the firm;
- they may simply enjoy the interaction between design and the physical production of a building.

However, a certain level of profitability is required if a firm in private practice is to remain viable and, although it is unlikely that profit *maximization* is sought by many in reality (most people could work an extra hour if maximization was the real objective), profit does act as a representative measure in a variety of reasons for being in practice. It can, for example, represent success, facilitate doing other things outside of work, and provide food and housing.

Thus, although profit, and certainly the maximization of profit, is unlikely to be the only objective for anyone, it does on the other hand have value as a representative measure of several aspects of people's needs.

1.1.2 Profit as a margin

Profit at the simplest level is the difference between the firm's income and the costs associated with earning that income.

Traditionally professional firms considered their income to be allocated in three broadly equal parts:

1. Overheads, such as accommodation, support staff, etc.
2. Salaries to professional staff.
3. Residue for partners.

A more realistic split is generally considered to be 40%, 40% and 20% in the order given above. The last of these items, residue for partners, is often termed profit but in fact is quite a complex item. Strictly speaking it includes at least three elements:

1. 'Salaries' to the partners for the work they do.
2. A return on the capital invested in the firm by the partners.
3. What is sometimes termed 'pure' profit after payment of the above two items.

It can be difficult to assess 'pure' profit, although this can be done roughly by ignoring the return to capital employed and assuming notional salaries to the partners based on reasonable levels of pay in the profession for those just below partnership level. The residue is approximately equal to 'pure' profit.

1.1.3 Profit as a comparative measure

Because profit is assessed in money terms it can usefully be used as a comparative measure between different firms, although this must be done carefully. It is essential that notional salaries are ascribed to the partners in a study that takes this approach, otherwise the partners will provide themselves with large salaries when the firm does well, small salaries when the firm is doing badly and the 'pure' profit will always be zero!

Another problem when making comparisons between firms is that their sizes vary and it is unrealistic to expect a small firm to make as much profit as a large firm, other things being equal. Thus, in making comparisons it is necessary to calculate a ratio that takes out the effect of size, such as **'pure' profit over income**. Thus the firm's profitability is assessed as a percentage of its income for the given year. This is the measure of profitability used in the research (Barrett, 1989), the results of which are drawn upon below and given in greater detail in Chapter 10. In this study of 36 firms of architects, surveyors and engineers, profit/income was found to vary from 2.5 to 20%.

Two questions therefore arise: What caused this spread in profitability? What were the major determinants?

1.2 INFLUENCES ON PERFORMANCE

A surprisingly common formula in the management texts is $P = f(a, m)$, where P = performance, a = ability and m = motivation. This applies to individuals and conveys the message that the performance of an individual is a function of that person's ability and motivation.

This doubtless applies to staff within professional firms involved in construction, but, given the people-intensive nature of professional firms, it seems valid to suggest that the equation applies in aggregate terms to the professional **firm as a whole**. Most people would readily agree that the members of a firm are its most important asset. The situation can be contrasted with a manufacturing-based organization where the production line and its attendant technology form the primary focus and the human workforce play a supporting role. Taken to an extreme, in process industries there may be very few staff operating vast plants.

So, for the professional firm it is suggested that its performance is primarily dependent on some summation of the staff's **abilities** they bring to bear on the problems confronting the firm, and their **motivation**. In a sense it seems that in managing a professional firm the key achievements necessary for success are to match staff of requisite ability to the tasks taken on by the firm and at the same time to do this in such a way that the same staff remain highly motivated. These twin objectives are not always compatible and the problem is likely to be highly fluid, changing from time to time and from person to person.

Taking this to an extreme, Figure 1.1 suggests the relationship in which the firm acts as a broker/facilitator between individual professionals and the clients.

The above discussion gives us two main areas in which to look for explanations of high performance. The first is matching staff to tasks – which revolves around a consideration, of abilities – and the second focuses on providing stimulation to elicit motivation. To take the discussion forward it is necessary to consider (a) those parts of the firm about which the managers can make decisions and (b) the variety of contexts within which firms operate.

1.3 MAIN PARTS OF THE PROFESSIONAL FIRM

As stated above, the major part of the firm is the people who make it up. These can be divided into **managers** and **staff**. The exact line to be drawn depends on

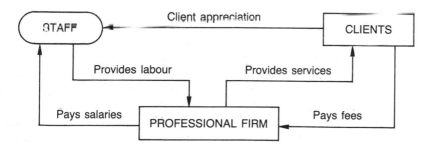

Fig. 1.1 The firm as facilitator between staff and clients

definitions, and the key here is to think in terms of functions rather than individuals.

Managers have been defined as people who decide what to do and then get **others** to do it. The essence of management is getting work done through other people and so it seems reasonable to consider managerial functions to be those that are not fee earning. From this perspective it can be seen that many people in professional firms are in fact part-time managers as some of their work involves long-term planning, marketing or supervision of other staff, but they also engage in fee-earning work and when they are doing this they can be considered to be 'staff'.

Looking beyond the people in the firm as individuals, we can consider the various ways in which they are grouped or allowed to specialize, and in this way the **structure** of the firm emerges. However, in addition to the firm's structure it is likely that the potential of the staff will be enhanced by the firm providing various types of **technology**. Obvious examples are word processors, moisture meters and software for structural calculations. This type of **machine technology**, generally speaking, makes it possible for staff to do their work more flexibly in terms of time, space and substance.

Although 'machine technology' is important for a professional firm, the knowledge it has and the way this knowledge is nurtured and used is of critical importance. Individuals within the firm will have knowledge, but the **knowledge technology** of the firm is a separate issue. It will include things such as checklists, standard drawings, standard specifications, proformas, etc. Its value can be clearly seen if you think of new people joining a firm to do a type of work of which they have little experience – say, housing association refurbishments – but which the firm has done for years. These individuals will be able to adopt the firm's 'knowledge technology' and almost immediately be effective at the type of work in question.

So the main factors that the firm can control are: the people involved, the way they are structured and the technology made available to them.

1.4 THE FIRM'S ENVIRONMENT

A common mistake in the past has been to base the discussion only on the above **internal** factors. Like many things that are critically important, once stated it should be patently obvious that it is necessary to consider the **context** within which the firm operates if sensible judgements are to be made regarding the internal factors. For example, the level of experience of staff is obviously important, but cannot be considered in isolation. To have someone who is very eminent in the field of planning law is of no consequence if it is not relevant to the type of work done by the firm. Alternatively, it is conceivable that two firms could have staff with very similar levels of experience, but one may engage in the design of very straightforward agricultural sheds, while the other may work on highly serviced clean rooms for computer manufacture.

Differences in the environment of professional firms is thus an important part of any discussion focused on how they should be managed, and it is helpful to divide up the external factors by differing time perspectives. For instance, there are long-term issues, say five to ten years in the future, about which the firm must make judgements. There are medium-term matters of a general nature which range from the 'here and now' to say one to two years in the future. Typically these would involve managing the client base with the objective of turning contacts and possibilities into actual projects. Lastly, there is that part of the firm's environment which impinges directly on the firm in the form of its current workload. It will comprise a stream of projects handled by the firm's staff.

1.5 MODEL OF THE PROFESSIONAL FIRM

We now have a variety of internal factors about which managers can make choices and a view of the firm's environment within which those decisions are taken. An outline model of how the various factors interrelate is given in Figure 1.2. The next section discusses how the model has been used to explain the differences in profitability noted earlier in this chapter.

1.6 A CONTINGENCY APPROACH

It is common in the field of management to hope for, perhaps even expect, universal solutions. This is possibly a reaction to the real life complexity of the problems leading to a yearning for someone to provide relatively simple answers. Many of the best-selling management books seek to satisfy this need, but it is questionable whether simple solutions are of much help.

Take a practical example with which most people involved in the construction industry can relate. A few years ago there was a rash of people specifying 1 : 3 (cement/sand) mortar for any and all circumstances. This inevitably led to problems, with the mortar shrinking back and dropping out as a whole when the background was too weak, or possibly damaging the brickwork. More expert professionals followed the guidance of the Building Research Establishment and would specify a mortar of similar strength to the background, using, say, 1 : 3 for engineering bricks below DPC or for sills and copings. For general facing brickwork they would specify a 1 : 1 : 6 gauged mortar mix, and for relatively weak internal blockwork, something like a 1 : 3 : 12 mix.

In a technical situation it is patently obvious that the choice between alternatives must be made in the **context** of surrounding factors. This occurs time and again. Think of soil types for foundations or the available means of support for roof structures. The approach taken is almost inevitably what is termed a **contingency approach**. That is to say, the solution chosen is contingent on other factors (Kast and Rosenzweig, 1981; Barrett, 1990b).

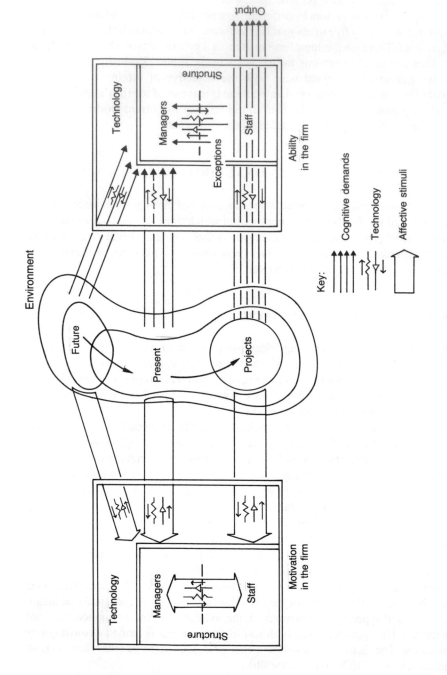

Fig. 1.2 Model of the professional firm

If this is true when we are dealing with inanimate pieces of timber, lumps of concrete and steel beams, when the most problematic factor to handle is the unpredictability of the weather, then how much more is this approach needed in any management analysis that will inevitably involve people? People's views, abilities and inclinations can vary from day to day, or from minute to minute. If a contingency approach is accepted it implies a more complex view in which alternatives are developed depending on contingent factors, but it is important not to see this as a deterministic process in which solution A is always appropriate in situation X and solution B is always appropriate in situation Y. There are a whole host of variables for the manager of the professional firm to play with and it is entirely possible that the desired result can be achieved quite satisfactorily using different combinations of the factors in different ways. This is confirmed by common experience of highly successful firms with radically different approaches to their management. Such a situation is a manifestation of **equifinality**, which is to say that although firms may start from different positions or travel by different routes, there is no reason why they should not achieve the same objective of high performance.

A very fluid picture has emerged in which the manager of the professional firm is seeking to make **appropriate** decisions using various internal factors about which he or she has choice while taking into account external influences. An understanding of these variables and the possible combinations should greatly increase the manager's ability to develop solutions tailored to the circumstances of a particular firm, and the remainder of this book is aimed at enhancing that understanding. But will such an understanding help increase profitability?

1.7 EXPLANATION OF DIFFERENCES IN PROFITABILITY

Before looking at the various factors in some detail, we are now in a position to return to the task of explaining the profit variations between firms studied in the research mentioned at the start of this chapter.

Using the model given in Figure 1.2, the management of these firms was assessed for appropriateness along the various interactions, including task management in the context of the firms' projects and in broader context, but also including staff management in the context of the known characteristics of professionals. The measures of appropriateness were then combined and found to explain 87% of the variation in profitability among the firms studied.

This confirms the importance of including a full range of factors and of looking for a fit between actions and circumstances.

For more details of the research underpinning the above brief statements, see Chapter 10.

The next two parts of this book will look in more detail at effective management in a range of situations.

PART TWO

Managing the firm's tasks

Managing ability | 2

2.1 WHAT IS ABILITY?

There are various ways of viewing this issue, but for practical purposes it is what people actually **do** that is important rather than what they are theoretically **capable** of doing. Thus, the definition of an individual's **ability** extends beyond consideration of the knowledge and skill base that an individual possesses, which might be said to define their **competence**. Most people will have come across individuals, often recently qualified, who have full command of the theory for a particular area, but are simply not sufficiently **confident** to act decisively. In these circumstances their ability to do the job is undermined. Nor is it unusual to find individuals at the other extreme – that is, they are hyper-confident, but in reality have no real idea of what needs to be done.

For the following discussion **ability** will be considered as an individual's worth judged against a particular task, based on some combination of the individual's confidence and competence to do the job.

This behavioural perspective means that one way of gaining a measure of an individual's ability for a particular task is to observe how much that individual requires support from superiors either in terms of technical inputs to make up for a lack of competence or sociometric support to make up for a lack of confidence. This links with the leadership model discussed in Chapter 7.

2.2 ABILITY PROFILE FOR PROFESSIONALS

A study based on responses from 684 individual professionals from the disciplines of architecture, engineering and surveying used the above approach to measure differences in ability levels against various factors, such as length of experience (Barrett, 1992). In the wide range of variables tested, the following were found to have a notable effect for some if not all of the worktypes:

- experience of the worktype in question;
- number of years qualified;
- number of firms worked for.

Table 2.1 Multiple correlation coefficients for ability by worktype

Worktypes	R	R × R (Adj)	Const (C)	Exp.[†]	Natural logarithms of Other exp.	Years qual.	No. firms
A1	0.776	0.593	2.039		0.558		
B1	0.830	0.673	1.947		0.323	0.338	
Q1	0.705	0.467	2.400	0.134	0.336		
E1	0.692	0.460	2.655	0.369			
A2	0.657	0.405	2.617	0.192	0.255		
B2	0.717	0.503	1.403			0.763	
Q2	0.616	0.361	3.059	0.301			
E2	0.401	0.132	2.598	0.279			
A3	0.704	0.482	2.681	0.409			
B3	0.788	0.603	1.851	0.334		0.388	
Q3	0.721	0.490	2.468	0.240			0.457
E3	0.715	0.496	2.527	0.434			
A4	0.683	0.454	0.936			0.820	
B4	0.788	0.612	2.112		0.582		
Q4	0.555	0.289	2.340	0.370			
E4	0.686	0.454	2.720	0.406			
A5	0.458	0.191	1.956			0.501	
B5	0.726	0.516	2.821	0.403			
Q5	0.665	0.426	2.743	0.391			
E5	0.768	0.576	2.234	0.551			
A6	0.669	0.420	2.150	0.250	0.330		
B6	0.672	0.425	2.121	0.367			0.508
Q6	0.576	0.313	2.242	0.443			
E6	0.604	0.344	2.893	0.359			
A7	0.782	0.593	2.006	0.256	0.333		
B7	0.691	0.465	2.561	0.628			
Q7	0.499	0.227	2.366	0.450			
E7	0.569	0.278	1.793			0.778	−0.668
A8	0.564	0.301	2.813	0.344			
B8	0.575	0.315	2.607	0.455			
Q8	0.759	0.550	1.292	0.460		0.342	
E8	0.559	0.290	2.676	0.398			
A9	0.806	0.632	0.392	0.318		0.754	
B9	0.763	0.564	1.628	0.386	0.440		
Q9	0.789	0.560	1.030	0.439		0.562	
E9	0.547	0.275	2.463	0.464			
A10	0.848	0.706	1.947	0.414			0.421
B10	0.709	0.480	2.035	0.255			0.647
Q10	0.797	0.625	2.564	0.425			
E10	0.522	0.249	1.407			0.595	

*Worktypes: A=Architects, B=Building Surveyors. Q=Quantity Surveyors and E=Structural Engineers; Nos 1–10 refer to specific worktypes by discipline and are described in Table 2.2.
[†] 'Exp'=experience in given discipline.
All entries significant at 0.05 level.

Table 2.2 Codes to worktypes in Table 2.1

Ref.	A	B	Q	E
Construction work				
1	New-build flats	Residential refurb.	Local auth. res. refurb.	New-build steel
2	Local auth. refurb.	Local auth. resid. refurb.	Commercial fit. out	New-build concrete
3	Commercial new-build	Commercial refurb.	Industrial new-build	Site invest./ founds
4	Industrial new-build	Industrial refurb.	M and E services	Residential alterations
5	Commercial fitting out	New-build project	Civil engineering	New-build bridge
Other work				
6	Structural survey	Structural survey	Structural survey	Structural survey
7	Development layouts	B. Society valuations	Life-cycle costing	Forensic engineer
8	Interior design	Dilapidations	Tax advice, etc.	Roads/ hardstanding
9	Expert witness	Expert witness	Expert witness	Expert witness
10	Practice management	Practice management	Practice management	Practice management

A further indicator that was also included related to the context of direct experience – that is, whether the respondent had experience of a broad variety of worktypes in addition to the subject worktype.

Table 2.1 gives the summary results from a regression analysis and shows the salient factors for a wide range of worktypes. Table 2.2 provides details of the coded worktypes in Table 2.1.

The results in Table 2.1 are difficult to show diagrammatically (in two dimensions) because, generally, more than two variables are involved, typically the dependent variable (ability) and two or three independent variables. However, in the case of structural engineers and structural surveys (E6), for instance, there are only two variables and the relationship described by this equation is shown in Figure 2.1. The rapid increase in ability in the first few years is clearly evident with the rate of improvement flattening out as complete competence is approached. Figure 2.2 shows the raw data as a scatterplot, and from this it is evident that inexperienced professionals are not only less able but their ability levels are much less predictable than later, when, as experienced people, they are more capable and more predictable. In Table 2.1 it will be seen that natural logarithms have been used to reflect the diminishing returns effect illustrated in Figure 2.1.

It can be seen from Table 2.1 that direct experience of the particular worktype in question is the most prevalent variable to emerge from the analysis. This in itself

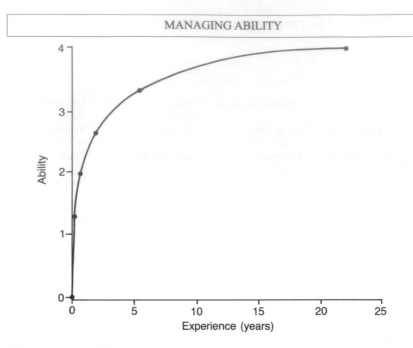

Fig. 2.1 Typical ability curve

is not surprising, but what was unexpected was the much lower incidence of general experience as an important variable. This factor is represented by the number of years qualified experience (ln) in the table. These findings provide support for Sibson's (1971) model of ability development, where an individual's overall ability is shown to rise as more tasks are mastered, but **each task** retains its own learning curve.

With number of years qualified representing the individual's quantity of experience, 'other experience' gives a measure of the diversity of the context experience. It can be seen that it is almost invariably one of these two variables that arises to complement the task specific experience. The number of firms worked for is the least prevalent variable, but interestingly occurs for two out of four of the disciplines in relation to managing the practice (A10 and B10).

In summary, it can be seen that there are generally multiple determinants of ability, each subject to diminishing returns (hence the use of logarithms) and, very importantly, ability levels are largely **task specific**. This last accords with common sense but is often overlooked. For instance, just because a partner is a superb architect or surveyor does not necessarily mean that he or she will be good at, say, practice management, or possibly the use of information technology. There is a tendency to treat people with a broad brush irrespective of significant differences. This is, of course, bound up with issues of status, pride, etc., but can lead to wholly inappropriate decisions and actions.

Although the analysis shows the different ability levels of a number of individuals at different stages of their careers it can be used as a surrogate for the way in

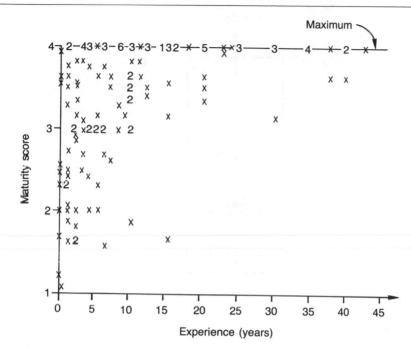

Fig. 2.2 Typical scatterplot of ability against experience

which a single individual's ability might be expected to vary during his or her career.

It has not been possible to explain the detailed variations in independent variables between worktypes and disciplines, as this requires much further work. However, we now have an understanding of the ways in which ability **tends** to vary. The next section will show the pervasive effects of different levels of ability among staff.

2.3 IMPLICATIONS FOR PRACTICE

On the typical ability profile shown above it is notable that the score for indicating total competence and confidence to do a given task is not reached for some time. So, how does a firm cope with, possibly, a high proportion of staff operating with insufficient ability to do the jobs presented to them? This is not a trivial question and obviously most firms overcome the problem one way or another. Some understanding of the range of possibilities and how they interrelate is critical to positive management rather than the mere continuation of customs and practices because they seemed to have worked in the past. Tried and tested procedures are to be greatly valued but their benefits should be fully understood and critically assessed if maximum performance is sought.

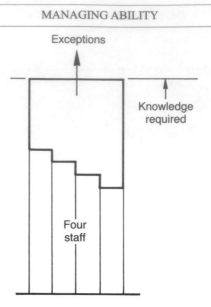

Fig. 2.3 The ability gap

2.3.1 The ability gap

A common way to deal with the discrepancy between the ability level required to do a job and the levels possessed by staff has been termed **hierarchical referral**. Simply stated, the subordinate asks someone more senior, who tells him the answer so that he can continue working until he comes across the next problem when he has to ask again. Figure 2.3 shows the situation described above, that is, a horizontal line some distance above a base line defines the level of ability **required** for a particular job. Four members of staff are shown with varying levels of ability (represented by the heights of the bars), but all fall short of the level required to do the particular job. The space between the 'knowledge required' line and the tops of the bars represents the magnitude of the **ability gap**.

A large ability gap will indicate that many questions are being put to superiors, whereas a small ability gap will mean that few questions are being asked.

Before looking at alternative ways of dealing with this ability gap we shall continue our consideration of the obvious reaction already mentioned – namely, hierarchical referral.

2.3.2 Hierarchical referral

To take an extreme situation, consider an unusual type of firm which has, however, existed at various times in recent years. This firm comprises a number of highly qualified professionals who operate in separate geographical locations almost as sole principals, but they do share a name, indemnity insurance, and some limited accounting procedures. It should be apparent that in this situation the ability gap

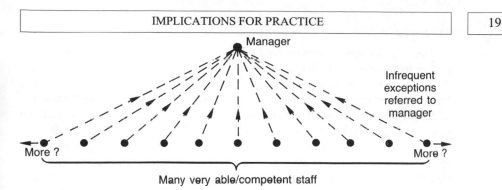

Manager

Infrequent
exceptions
referred to
manager

More ?

More ?

Many very able/competent staff

Fig. 2.4 Structure generated by high ability staff

in each instance is very small if not non-existent. Each member is capable of carrying out his or her own affairs without reference to the other 'partners' in the firm. That is not to say that some benefit is not obtained through a certain amount of cross-referencing on particularly difficult problems, but in general there are few **exceptions**. The organizational structure for this firm is shown in Figure 2.4.

It can be seen that the organization is flat in the extreme, in fact it could well be a hierarchy of one level, unless there was a desire to coordinate for the sake of consistency across the organization, in which case it might be a hierarchy of two levels as shown. In this instance there is really very little need for a hierarchy at all.

A structure like this can seem ideal, but does have drawbacks in that inevitably the highly qualified individuals will end up dealing with some aspects of their work that is well beneath their abilities unless they have a positive strategy, successfully implemented, of taking only projects demanding high technical expertise. So, there is the danger of wasted resources due to a lack of hierarchy.

At the other extreme, there are a number of very large firms where professionally qualified staff are the exception rather than the rule and there is a high proportion of unqualified or trainee staff. The situation in a firm like this has been typified by Maister (1982) as shown in Figure 2.5.

In a firm like this, because the staff 'grinding' at the workface are not well qualified they demand supervision to cope with the exceptions generated – that is, the questions they ask – which are handled by the 'minders'.

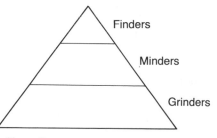

Finders

Minders

Grinders

Fig. 2.5 Possible structure of large firm

The 'finders' are fully employed obtaining work which, as far as possible, is known to be suited to the limited abilities of the 'grinders'.

It is useful at this stage to consider the concept of **span of control** which has long been used in organizational design. The span of control represents the number of people that an individual can effectively supervise. There has long been debate as to what this number should be; should it be 3, 5, or possibly 7? The truth is, of course, that it depends on the ability gap for which the supervisor is responsible. If the subordinates are of limited ability but the work is extremely straightforward then the supervisor may have a span of control of 20, but if something goes radically wrong then this can immediately drop to a span of control of 1 while he takes over and sorts out a problem (Sibson, 1971). In a situation with the same staff but relatively difficult work the span of control may be, say, 3. A typical span of control in a professional firm is probably 6 or 7. These differences may sound small, but taking a firm of around 50 professional staff the implications for the number of managers required are pronounced. With a span of control of 1 : 20, three managers are needed, if it drops to 1 : 6, then about ten managers and at 1 : 3, 18 managers.

Although, of course, managers ('people getting work done through other people') are inevitably more senior and therefore 'important', it is necessary to remember that, by the definition of 'manager' given in Chapter 1, they are not fee earning. That is, they are an overhead – a cost. In the firm with a span of control of 3, the fee-earning staff comprise only 64% of the total workforce. The remainder, typically drawing higher salaries, are not directly fee earning when acting in their managerial roles as opposed to staff roles.

Although there is the question of obtaining leverage within a firm by using billing rates for senior staff while getting the work done by cheaper junior members of the firm (Maister, 1982) it seems clear that, where **unnecessarily incurred**, hierarchical referral is an expensive way of handling the ability gap. This is not to say that hierarchical referral is not an appropriate reaction in many circumstances, but the alternatives should be considered and the relative costs and benefits should be analysed before it is accepted as the automatic mechanism to fill the ability gap confronting the firm.

Some other means by which the ability gap can be closed can now be considered.

2.3.3. Using technology and structure

It was mentioned in Chapter 1 that, in addition to 'people', managers within professional firms can also make choices about the structure of the firm and the use made of technology.

It was suggested that in the professional firm **knowledge technology** is every bit as important as the machinery usually brought to mind by the word 'technology', and this suggestion has been clearly demonstrated in Figure 2.6.

Knowledge technology within the firm is knowledge the **firm** possesses as opposed to particular individuals, and this encoded knowledge can be released to members of the firm to assist them in their work. Through this mechanism the need

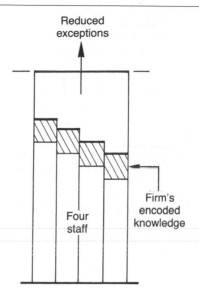

Fig. 2.6 The effect of encoded knowledge

to ask a superior in an exception situation can be greatly reduced – that is, the ability gap can be closed. This is indicated by the hatched area in Figure 2.6, which has reduced the size of the ability gap.

As far as the use of structure is concerned, one method has already been discussed, namely, hierarchical referral; however, there are other mechanisms, one of which has already been alluded to in the example of the firm with a number of highly qualified staff. Here the value of an interchange of ideas between people with not vastly dissimilar ability levels was stressed and it is common experience that in any group each person will know something that some other members of the group do not. It is through this exchange mechanism that groups of peers can absorb problems without the need to refer to the next level of hierarchy. This is shown diagrammatically in Figure 2.7 and represents the lateral absorption of problems through team work. Thus, the lines between the four individuals within the firm have become dashed to indicate that they are no longer isolated and can exchange views freely. The isolation previously implied is quite simple to create. It does not have to mean geographical separation in separate towns, but can be created by something as simple as separate buildings, or staircases between areas of the office, or even space separated into small offices rather than open plan. Again, if this exchange mechanism can be encouraged, the size of the ability gap can be reduced.

The third and last way in which structure can be used revolves around the choice of who does what type of work – that is, the key word is **specialization**. By allowing people to specialize, typically through the creation of departments, a firm can lower the ability level required by narrowing the range of issues with which any individual

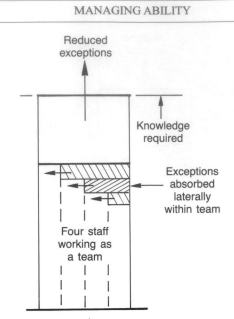

Fig. 2.7 Use of structure: teamwork

has to deal. This is indicated in Figure 2.8 and can, again, significantly reduce the ability gap.

The specialization can be by major **worktype** where the technical demands are significantly different. For example, housing as compared with science parks.

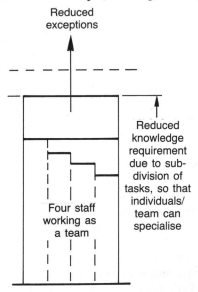

Fig. 2.8 Use of structure: specialization

Another criterion can be **client type** where it is in fact the demands of the client bodies that differ more radically than the technical aspects of the projects – for example, private individuals compared with Ministry of Defence work. Lastly, the specialization can be driven by an internal subdivision of **tasks** rather than some market subdivision, for example, contract administration compared with producing scheme designs.

2.4 DISCUSSION

So, the concept of the firm's ability gap enables technology and structure to be seen as **alternative** means of reducing the volume of exceptions referred up the hierarchy of the firm.

The magnitude of the 'gap' will depend on the demands of the firm's projects and the relevant abilities of staff. Maister categorizes projects into:

- 'brains' requiring one-off problem solving ;
- 'grey hairs' requiring experience;
- 'procedure' requiring efficient systems and procedures.

He argues that project teams with decreasing proportions of senior to junior staff are required as you go down the list, driven mainly by hierarchical considerations. This is a useful way of describing one aspect of the situation, but there are other salient factors.

The extent to which technology, specialization and teamwork are employed to complement hierarchical referral will depend on senior management's judgement. Many factors need to be taken into account if **appropriate** responses are to be identified (e.g. Barrett, 1991). It is necessary for managers within specific professional practices to make judgements based on their local situation as to the relative costs and benefits of the alternative measures, and to then make a choice as to the optimum arrangement for their firm. However, the main considerations are summarized below.

Briefly, if the firm's flow of work is repetitive, the use of knowledge technology – such as checklists, standard documents, specialist programs – may well be a sound reaction, but may lead to demotivation if standardization is imposed rather than the encoded knowledge being made available to staff as a resource.

Specialization can be effective if the firm has sufficient work of the given kind, but this approach can generate a need for coordination and may demotivate if the tasks created are too circumscribed. The use of part-time specialists is a common response.

Teamwork is only really possible in larger firms and demands highly effective informal communications if it is to be successful. Open plan offices, skilled team leaders can help, but individuals leaving can disrupt the dynamics of the team and lead to knowledge loss for the firm if there has been little encoding of procedures, etc.

The final alternative of hierarchical referral carries with it the cost of involving senior (and therefore expensive) members of the firm, but can enable them to pass on not only their knowledge, but also affective aspects such as their professionalism, in the broadest sense. Feedback to staff can also occur automatically with positive motivational connotations.

It can be seen that there are many factors at work. The concept of the **ability gap** can act as a focus when trying to decide which combination of alternatives to employ to balance the demands of the firm's work with the abilities of its staff.

A final point in this section is that the analysis can extend beyond the boundary of the firm. Knowledge technology can be 'bought in' from a specialist firm, so relieving the firm's own staff of the problem. For example, surveyors use structural engineers for the more complicated calculations. If this is done on a regular basis then it could be viewed as a structural response, using specialization. Depending on ownership of the practices, this could lead to the development of a multi-disciplinary practice.

2.5 BUILDING KNOWLEDGE

So far the discussion has been implicitly carried out at a point in time; the analysis has been cross-sectional. If consideration is now extended over time, in a longitudinal analysis, than in the light of the discussion so far it should be clear that if the firm can take action to improve the knowledge of its staff together with its own encoded knowledge, the benefits derived from a reduced ability gap would be very worth while.

This is, of course, closely linked to Continuing Professional Development (CPD), now a mandatory requirement for most construction professionals. This applies to individuals, but if their development can be linked to that of the firm, then it need not be seen as a cost as time lost to productive work, but rather as an

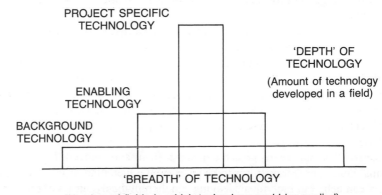

Fig. 2.9 Enabling technology

investment in the future. This mentality led one firm of architects to support staff to attend various seminars on 'clean rooms' for computer manufacture in order to support the agreed future direction of the firm into industrial construction for high technology companies.

Firms can also take positive action in how they **use** their workload to provide opportunities for improving the knowledge base of the firm as well as getting the work done. This can be made clearer through the use of the concept of **enabling technology**, which is distinguished from 'project specific' technology and the 'background' technology available to all firms (Figure 2.9).

If firms can develop plans that bring the firm's goals into line with the goals of its staff, and if the staff can link their learning with the development of **enabling technology** within the firm, then a very powerful resource will be created over time to the benefit of all.

2.6 THE ABILITY GAP AND ...

The above discussion has been entirely in terms of staff handling the projects of the firm; however, exactly the same factors are relevant at each linkage between the firm and its environment. Thus, demands are made on the partners of a firm both through their short- to medium-term interaction with their client base and through their long-term planning. Even in these instances there may be a mismatch between the demands placed on the individuals and their abilities to handle the issues, and, as with project work, the use of technology or structure will be necessary to close the ability gaps in these directions.

For example, until the last decade or so, within the UK, the construction professions enjoyed a stable environment with relatively well-understood relationships between the various professions and other participants in the industry as well as defined scale fees. Now all this has changed, and long-term planning has become very problematic opening up, in some cases, a considerable ability gap which some firms have endeavoured to close by importing knowledge through the employment of management consultants.

2.7 SUMMARY

A whole range of factors have been discussed and the common focus has been the ability gap. This depends on the balance between the demands being made by the work of the firm and the abilities of the staff to deal with the demands. Various possible reactions have been outlined. Encoded knowledge can be provided to staff or knowledge can be imported to the practice through other means. Or structure can be used through hierarchical referral, teamwork or specialization. The model applies to all interactions in which members of the firm use their ability to deal with problems. Extending consideration over time introduces the idea of consciously building enabling technology within the firm.

To complement the above discussion of the principles underlying the mechanisms through which problems can be absorbed by a firm, the following three chapters will look at the practical steps involved in the firm effectively dealing with strategic management, marketing and cost and time control.

2.8 CHECKLIST

Bearing in mind the expertise available within the firm and the level of difficulty of the technical and managerial tasks confronted:

- Does the firm use hierarchical referral excessively to absorb exceptions?
- Is there repetitive work which could be proceduralized and would repay the investment?
- Could steps be taken to facilitate the free flow of ideas and knowledge informally within the firm?
- Is there sufficient volume of particular worktypes to justify specialization within the firm?
- Is there an explicit policy to identify material from specific projects that can be used as 'enabling technology' for future projects?
- Are positive efforts made to link the development of staff (and managers) with the desired direction of the firm as a whole?
- Does the firm have specific problem areas (technical or managerial) for which it should buy in expertise from outside of the firm?

Strategic management | 3

3.1 WHAT IS STRATEGIC MANAGEMENT?

Strategic management has been called various things by various people. Some people term it corporate planning, others strategic management, but the key facet of this activity is the quest for major decisions that affect the whole of the organization and its long-term relationship with its business environment.

Over recent years there have been many studies that tend to indicate that organizations do not in fact produce and follow long-term plans, but instead tend to operate more intuitively. As with most things the situation is more complex than this and an organization's journey from its intended strategy to what it actually does has been summarized as shown in Figure 3.1.

We cannot discuss definitions in detail here, but a useful paper by Dadfar and Gustavssan (1989) reviews the different standpoints in more detail for those who are interested. Suffice it to say that the **intended strategy** has a part to play, although the strategy determined may not be realized in full.

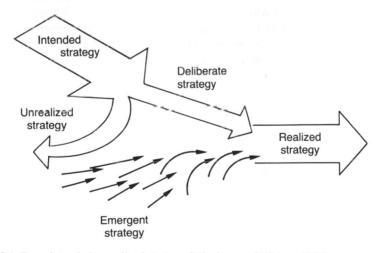

Fig. 3.1 From intended to realized strategy (Minzberg and Waters, 1985)

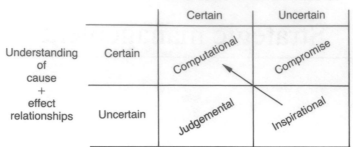

Fig. 3.2 Decision making and uncertainty (Thompson, 1967)

3.2 VALUE OF STRATEGIC MANAGEMENT

One way of portraying the benefit that can be gained from the strategic management **process** is given in Figure 3.2. From this figure it can be seen that understanding the cause and effect relationships attached to alternatives – that is, what would **actually** happen if you made a given decision – is one dimension of the uncertainty surrounding decision making, but in addition there is another dimension, and this is the extent to which a **consensus** is achieved among those making the decision. It is in this latter area that the strategic management process can be very beneficial in bringing issues out into the open and moving the organization towards a consensus, both in terms of what the organization is aiming to achieve and how it hopes to get there. In this way the firm can align the efforts of the various participants in the organization to be mutually supportive.

One way of showing this orientation and the effect it can have on re-aligning subsidiary decisions within the firm is given in Figure 3.3. A well-known example where this relationship is often overlooked with disastrous results is a firm's approach to investing in computer technology. Without a strong framework, incompatibility is almost certain to arise between different types of software, hardware and combinations of these components.

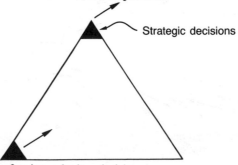

Fig. 3.3 Alignment of major and minor decisions

Another key consideration is that the process of strategic management forces those involved to take on an external orientation. It shifts attention away from parochial squabbles and emphasizes the importance of the business environment, with which the firm must mesh effectively if it is to survive. This perspective is backed up by a certain amount of research in relation to construction firms. For instance, Carlisle (1987) came to the conclusion that the firms that engaged in strategic management performed better, not necessarily because they had made particular decisions, but principally because the process of strategic management had created an external orientation within the firm. Coxe *et al.* (1987) adduce some tentative evidence that those professional firms involved in the US construction industry that have focused efforts around their strengths have been more successful.

The strategic management process does not have to be extremely formal and some researchers (Kotter, 1982) have concluded that successful managers develop rough **agendas** of things they would like to achieve and simultaneously work up **networks** of colleagues and external contacts through whom they can endeavour to make progress. In principle, this approach is very similar to formal strategic planning in that the object is to overcome a pervasive organization problem, namely 'the triumph of the urgent over the important'.

There is often debate as to whether strategic management is suitable for small firms. If the possibility of strategic management being pursued formally or informally is accepted, it is then only a small step to suggest that it is appropriate for big and small firms; however, in either case the information should be recorded, at least in summary form, in order to focus the mind and confirm commitment.

The benefits to firms of different sizes can be illustrated by analogy with matters maritime. Large tankers, with their massive momentum, need to plan ahead in order to change direction before it is too late. In contrast a small dingy, which can change direction instantly, needs to know where it is ultimately going in order to remain on course. Only in the worse conditions does the captain give up control to the elements; and even in this case, only by planning ahead and scanning the horizon, might it have been possible to avoid the storm altogether. So, to the extent that the analogy holds true it can be seen that longer term plans can perform a useful function irrespective of the size of the organization.

3.3 MAJOR FEATURES OF STRATEGIC MANAGEMENT

We shall now briefly look at how this type of management differs from others, the relevant time scale and level of detail and, lastly, who should do it.

3.3.1 What is special about strategic management?

Most decisions made within a firm are concerned with specifics and can very often be made in quite considerable detail. In the case of strategic management the whole process is designed to identify a relatively small grouping of major factors and to make some critical decisions about the overall direction of the firm. Argenti (1980) says it is 'planning for the wood not the trees' or 'planning for the firm as a whole, not the whole of the firm'.

This second quotation focuses attention on the potential difficulty of the process if it is thought that it involves making **all** the decisions for the firm at **all** levels. The key to keeping the process manageable is the realization that it is only decisions that effect the **whole** of the firm that are to be considered. These few major decisions lead to the general thrust of the firm and if they are wrong then the quality of subsidiary decisions can be irrelevant.

In this context it is useful to introduce the distinction between **effectiveness** and **efficiency**. **Effectiveness** relates to whether the firm is moving into the correct longer term markets, whereas **efficiency** depends on whether the firm's current operations are as cost-effective as possible. As an example, it is instructive to look back over the last ten years. A decade ago many building surveying firms had become highly efficient at processing local authority and housing association work, but were badly hit when public sector funding diminished rapidly. The firms have managed their environment efficiently, but not effectively. Ten years later many of these firms have diversified strongly into commercial work, a sector that had performed strongly, but they have again been badly hit as this market has also collapsed. Similar examples could be drawn for architects and engineers. The point is that the strategic management process, if handled properly, can give firms an **outward** and **forward-looking** perspective, so that major changes can be anticipated and, at least, accommodated if not capitalized upon.

3.3.2 Time-scale

Strategic management has a long-term perspective – but what is 'long term'? Let us take a time frame of five to ten years. It is not critical to be more accurate providing consideration is drawn beyond annual budgeting and the three-year financial plans that some companies keep. It is necessary for those involved to be drawn into speculating about what might happen beyond the easy comfort of the immediate future. This is not to say that the plans settled upon will last right through to the planning horizon. They should be reviewed periodically, and when the senior members of the firm lose confidence in them, the plans should, of course, be revised.

The objective of the process is, however, to produce robust general guidelines that are not undermined by changes at a day-to-day level.

3.3.3 Level of detail

The appropriate level of detail could be described as 'sketchy' and the logic behind this is summarized in Figure 3.4. In this figure it can be seen that the 'sketchy' level of detail is merely an acknowledgement of the longer time frame, and as the firm implements the plans down to an everyday level, more detail will be added.

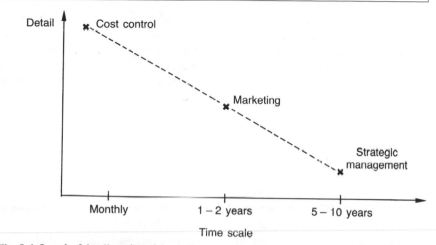

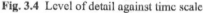

Fig. 3.4 Level of detail against time scale

3.3.4 Who should do the planning?

It is self-evident that the top managers should be involved in the strategic management process. It is not something that the top *person* – be it senior partner, chief executive, etc. – can step aside from. Unless he or she is involved, the decisions that are made are unlikely to be fully accepted and implemented within the firm.

The question then arises 'How many other people should be involved?' – and for this type of decision making, involving difficult problems with important ramifications, there is strong support for the establishment of a group of four or five people working in a highly interactive way. In this way a spread of view points can be brought to bear, and ideas that emerge can be fully tested among peers. As a result the process is likely to be fairly time consuming, but this is justified by the importance of the process (see Figure 3.5).

Fig. 3.5 Appropriate communication patterns (Bevalas, 1950). The 'wheel' is good for relatively straightforward problems where speed is important, but the commitment and motivation of those on the rim is not. 'All-channel' communication is good for difficult problems, engenders high levels of commitment in those involved, but is time-consuming. The 'circle' alternative is inferior in all respects, but does arise in practice, for instance in a department with no central figure and few meetings attended by all. If this situation is identified and collaborative effort is required for goal accomplishment, then efforts should be made to move towards one of the other networks, with the choice dependent on the difficulty of the problem and the desire for commitment.

There is a potential problem with larger firms when the commitment of, say, 20 partners is desired, but to involve them all would make discussions unnecessarily unwieldy. In these circumstances, and in order to obtain commitment from junior staff in any event, it is possible to introduce parts of the process where everyone is involved in brainstorming sessions, etc., which then act as a source of ideas for the main planning group.

When the process relies only on the involvement of people from within the firm there is the potential danger that those at a senior level will have been conditioned through a process of socialization, such that, by the time they reach the top of the firm they may all tend to think in a very similar way. This can be very dangerous for the type of decision making involved in strategic management, but can be countered by the use of non-executive directors, management consultants or other people within the firm who are selected to give diversity to the planning group. This is not just a nice academic point. Lansley (1985), in a study of, admittedly, major contractors over ten years, found that those that had a spread of problem-solving approaches among their directors had been more profitable and had grown more than firms with homogenous senior management groups. Although this research concerned a different sort of business, the companies were coping with the same environment as the construction professions.

A model specifically focused on learning (in this context, problem-solving) styles is provided by Kolb (1976) and shown in Figure 3.6. This provides a vocabulary to discuss the issue of styles. Powell (1991) has applied this model to the construction professions and argues that individuals cannot realistically be

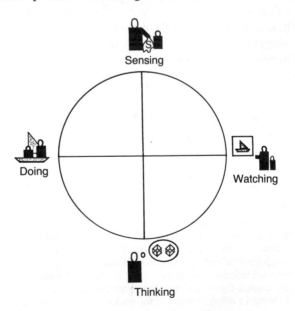

Fig. 3.6 Kolb's learning cycle

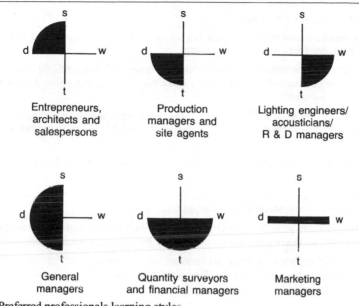

Fig. 3.7 Preferred professionals learning styles

equally strong on all four styles, **sensing**, then actively **watching**, **thinking** about what has been seen and then, lastly, **doing**. Further, to be effective decision makers under pressure of time, short cuts are used by **individuals** who, as a result, will run the risk of producing impaired decisions. For strategic, and therefore extremely important, decisions this is a big risk to take and so a **group**, which together has a balance of the four styles, is recommended.

To give a flavour of how Kolb's styles link with stereotypes for construction professionals, Powell's aggregate results for specific professional groups are given in Figure 3.7. The group Powell says he cannot understand is 'marketing managers' who appear to move from watching to doing without thinking!

A strategic management team with a complementary set of Kolb's styles would have the **potential** to handle the problems well, but if the necessary **team skills** are not present then this potential may not be realized. Belbin (1981) provides a well-known categorization of eight major team roles, as shown in Table 3.1. These need not each represent an individual; one person can perform more than one role, but for an effective team all are required.

3.3.5 Summary

We have now discussed why strategic management is important and what distinguishes it from other types of decision making within the professional firm in terms of timescale, level of detail and who should do it. The next section provides a step-by-step process model designed to generate sound strategies for the professional firm.

Table 3.1 Belbin's team roles

1. **Chairman** ensures that the best use is made of each member's potential. Is self-disciplined, dominant but not domineering.

2. **Shapers** look for patterns and try to shape the team's efforts in this direction. They are out going, impulsive and impatient. They make the team feel uncomfortable but they make things happen.

3. **Innovators** are the source of original ideas. They are imaginative and uninhibited. They are bad at accepting criticism and may need careful handling to provide that vital spark.

4. **Evaluators** are more measured and dispassionate. They like time to analyse and mull things over.

5. **Organizers** turn strategies into manageable tasks which people can get on with. They are disciplined, methodical and sometimes inflexible.

6. **Entrepreneurs** go outside the group and bring back information and ideas. They make friends easily and have a mass of contacts. They prevent the team from stagnating.

7. **Team workers** promote unity and harmony within a group. They are more aware of people's needs than other members. They are the most active internal communicators and cement of the team.

8. **Finishers** are compulsive 'meeters' of deadlines. They worry about what can go wrong and maintain a permanent sense of urgency which they communicate to others.

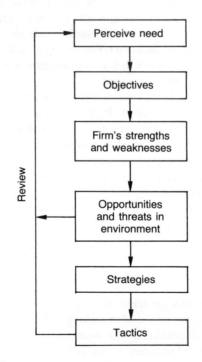

Fig. 3.8 The strategic management process

3.4 THE STRATEGIC MANAGEMENT PROCESS

The following is based in large part on Argenti's (1980) model. This comprises a series of steps, which are given in Figure 3.8.

3.4.1 Perception

Accomplishing the first stage, that is perceiving the need to review the strategic direction of the firm, is not a foregone conclusion. The discussion so far will hopefully have lent weight to the argument that such a review is worth while, especially if the alternative is to wait for a crisis, when both the resources and cool objectivity required are likely to be absent. If the firm has already instituted a strategic plan it may now have lost confidence in that plan and needs to go through the planning process again.

Given the desirability of including as many people as possible in at least some stages of the process, the overall process can take two or three months for a small firm of, say, ten staff and for a larger firm it could take from six to twelve months, depending on how much time people devote to it.

A process of this magnitude requires commitment, especially as the *status quo* is likely to be challenged, and so it is worth repeating that top management must be involved. In practical terms these people are likely to be very busy, and, to increase the chances of the process reliably continuing to completion it is advisable for someone to be appointed to act as the **clockwork** for the process. This person will be less senior, but must command general respect. Someone at about associate level will probably be most suitable.

3.4.2 Objectives

Once the process has started, the first major step is to determine the objectives of the firm. This may sound very straightforward, but if successfully performed this can be critical in achieving a consensus, which, as already mentioned above, is one of the main benefits that can flow from this process. The issue of objectives can be broken down into four components: ethos, mission statement, prioritized objectives/performance measures and gap analysis.

(a) Ethos

The ethos of the firm allows consideration of overriding constraints that the rest of the planning process will have to acknowledge. For instance, most firms would immediately exclude the use of slaves, racist activities and illegal operations! There may, however, be special circumstances affecting the firm, an example of which could be the Quaker firm with the chance to tender for the design of a brewery. A further type of constraint which may affect some professional firms could arise because they are part of a larger organization which itself sets boundaries within which the 'firm' must operate.

Many of these issues will not be treated explicitly in practice. There are two dangers to avoid. If there is a very strong implicit consensus this may make the practice blind to some perfectly sensible alternatives. The architectural firm that takes for granted that 'we only deal with the design of new buildings' severely limits its options. Conversely, if there are pronounced differences in ethos, but this is not discussed, then the remainder of the process will suffer from this in-built tension. For example, one partner who is driven solely by profit will eventually clash with another who feels that the firm has a responsibility to provide free services to disadvantaged members of society.

(b) Mission statement

Many people dismiss mission statements in that they are in a sense just a 'wish list'. However, there is the argument that the firm will be subject to constraints so that in the medium term (say five to ten years) it will have to prioritize its efforts, whereas in the long term (plus ten years) it would seek a whole range of achievements. By introducing a mission statement which encapsulates very long-term views it can be psychologically easier for those involved to say, 'That's what we would like to do, but because of X, Y and Z we have to be realistic'. In this way the mission statement can serve a useful purpose.

(c) Prioritized objectives/performance measures

This stage provides a concrete framework for the later development of strategies. Clearly, for the private practice firm profit is likely to figure prominently here. The managers of the firm may have strong views on size, either to grow or to remain small. There could be a strong commitment to provide long-term employment to staff. Building long-term goodwill might be chosen, and there may well be other objectives that make sense to the particular firm in question. Unless the objectives selected are **really** of equal weight, then they should be prioritized so that trade-offs can be clearly assessed later.

Identifying the objectives of the firm is likely to prove an effective mechanism for bringing the sort of underlying differences, already mentioned above, out into the open.

The next stage appears simple, but is really quite dangerous. It is to decide upon **measures** of performance. Through the choice of measures the objectives are operationalized. There is a danger that a measure will be chosen because it is easy to measure, rather than because it closely represents the objective in question. Etzioni (1964) termed this 'over-measurement' and unless care is taken the firm's efforts can be diverted away from its intended objectives.

In the not-for-profit sector some measures related to the core activity of the organization will be required, such as service to the community, but profit measures are increasingly being used even in this sector as a surrogate for efficiency.

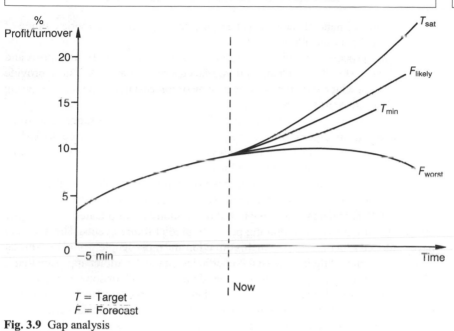

Fig. 3.9 Gap analysis

(d) Gap analysis

Once the measures have been chosen, the next stage is to pursue a gap analysis involving targets and forecasts **assuming no change in strategy**. The last statement is important because the idea of the gap analysis is to identify whether new strategies are required. It may be that the existing strategy – whether explicit or implied in a stream of past decisions – is perfectly sound. Figure 3.9 shows the gap analysis in graphical form. The measures used should be carefully chosen so that they can be tracked over time and ratios are often used for this purpose. For example, to represent profit the ratio profit/income is shown in the figure as a percentage.

The main elements to note are that you should go back as far as possible on historical data to extrapolate a trend for the given measure. Once this has been done it is necessary to project forward targets and forecasts. In both cases it is not realistic to expect to do this with a single line given the extended time frame involved. Rather a likely **range** is used which will tend to broaden as time goes on and judgements become less exact.

It was mentioned in Chapter 1 that people do not really maximize profit, but it is perfectly possible to think in terms of what would be a **satisfactory** level of performance (T_{sat}) and what is the **minimum** acceptable level of performance (T_{min}). The minimum level of performance clearly links with the opportunity cost of being in business. If you could get a better return by placing your investment in a building society, then it may be that staying in business is not a sensible decision if your only measure is financial success. Taken together, T_{sat} and T_{min} provide a range of performance that is acceptable.

A similar process is required for forecasts as to what is **likely** to happen and what is the **worst** that could happen if you faced a run of bad luck. These provide F_{likely} and F_{worst}, which together provide a range of forecast performance, **assuming no change in present strategy**.

In simple terms, if the forecast range falls below the target range then some reassessment of strategies is urgently required. If the ranges are coincident, existing strategies may well suffice. If the situation is as shown in Figure 3.9, then some reassessment of strategies is suggested in order to improve F_{worst}.

A difficult question is how best to make the forecasts and develop the targets. Viewed positively, this is another area where consensus within the firm can be developed. It is, of course, possible to build enormously complicated econometric models that use massive computing power to predict future events. The Treasury have deployed a lot of resources in this direction and most people would be familiar with the accuracy of their forecasts! Nevertheless, a much simpler approach that is likely to be accessible to most firms is the 'delphi' method, or some variant.

The essence of this method is that a number of 'experts' (say, the team set up to do the analysis) make estimates independently. The individuals then receive feedback of other people's estimates, after which they reconsider their judgements and the process continues iteratively in this fashion until a consensus projection is reached. For the type of measures being dealt with here this approach has been found to be really quite successful and, as already mentioned, it assists the development of a consensus within the firm, which in itself is valuable. Strictly speaking, when using the delphi method the individuals should not communicate directly and it is probably worth maintaining this in the early iterations, but more in-depth discussions within the group may be valuable once the broad parameters for the measures have been established.

Now that the objectives of the firm have been brought to life, the next stage in the strategic management process can start.

3.4.3 SWOT analysis

This stage is concerned with analysing the firm's Strengths and Weaknesses and the Opportunities and Threats it faces in its environment. This element of the process is increasingly well known and is commonly referred to as a SWOT analysis or a WOTS UP analysis!

The aim of this part of the process is to produce a relatively short list of the major factors that the firm ought to take into account when arriving at its strategies. There will normally be an initial step designed to generate a lot of **possible** factors to be considered, followed by a further step in which these are whittled down to the **major** factors.

Generating possible factors can be pursued in various ways. A free-flowing meeting of the whole of the firm could be held, possibly away from the place of work, for a large firm, perhaps using syndicate groups. It has been found that people come up with more ideas individually than in groups, although there is more potential to spark off ideas within a group. It therefore seems sensible to have an initial phase in the meeting where people work as individuals producing as many ideas as they can, which they then bring to a group discussion where further thoughts are stimulated.

It is important that the process allows for recording the ideas that arise otherwise the benefit can be lost. If it is difficult to get people together, this first step can be achieved by a questionnaire, which can be sent not only to members of the firm, but also to clients and other external people with whom the firm deals. These external views can be very useful in achieving an objective perspective, particularly of the firm's strengths and weaknesses.

The following factors have been collected during wide-ranging discussions about this firm's strategy for the future. Please rate each to indicate how important *you* think it is.

FACTORS	IMPORTANCE				
Strengths:	None	Little	Some	Very	Essential
Well-qualified staff	1	2	3	4	5
Experience of educational buildings	1	2	3	4	5
Etc.	1	2	3	4	5
Weaknesses:					
Lack of team spirit	1	2	3	4	5
Weak accounting systems	1	2	3	4	5
Etc.	1	2	3	4	5
Opportunities:					
Work in Europe	1	2	3	4	5
Work on repossessions	1	2	3	4	5
Etc.	1	2	3	4	5
Threats:					
Professional indemnity	1	2	3	4	5
Competition from other professionals	1	2	3	4	5
Etc.	1	2	3	4	5

Please give your name and position in the firm below:

———— - —————

———— - —————

———— - —————

... and please return the completed questionaire to SP by ..... at the latest.

Thank you

Fig. 3.10 Example questionnaire for rating SWOT factors

Once a large number of possible factors has been produced for each of the four categories (S W O T) the next stage is for someone to sift through them, amalgamating those that only appear different but are essentially the same, until a more concise list has been produced. From this list it is then necessary to select the major factors, and one way of doing this is to circulate a questionnaire asking people in the firm to rate the factors for importance on a five-point scale. An example is given in Figure 3.10.

The questionnaire can be distributed to all members of the firm or just to senior members. Alternatively, it could be analysed for various subgroupings in the firm if the managers would find this useful. Whichever approach is taken the group formulating the firm's strategic plan will then draw from the analysis of the questionnaires those factors that receive strong support. At this stage the other factors must be rejected, which is very hard to do, but remember that the aim of the process is to identify those major factors to be taken into account so that the whole problem is reduced to a magnitude that can be handled realistically. It is quite arbitrary, but five factors per category seems quite sufficient, although it may be that some grouping of more or less than five stands out from the remainder after the analysis of questionnaires and may become the obvious choice.

In grouping the external factors (O T) it may be useful to take into account a common formulation of a firm's environment which provides four main areas: political (including legal issues), economic, social and technical (P E S T).

Once the SWOT analysis is completed this signifies the end of the ground work necessary to underpin the development of soundly based strategies. By now the firm's objectives should have been clarified and a consensus view obtained on the major strengths, weaknesses, opportunities and threats. The development of strategies now proceeds to maximize strengths and opportunities and minimize weaknesses and threats, all in the context of achieving the objectives the firm has set.

3.4.4 Strategies

The firm must seek to identify a major strategy for its market position, which then provides a framework for the development of a more detailed marketing strategy covering the main markets with which the firm interacts. These externally oriented strategies should then be supported by a coherent set of strategies related to internal factors, namely: people (ability and motivation), technology (machine and knowledge), structure (formal and informal) and resources (money and premises).

Resulting from a major seminar in America, Coxe et al. (1987, pp. 37–45) produced a framework of 'success strategies' for construction professionals. This is shown in summary form in Figure 3.11 and may assist as a more detailed guide. It covers many of the areas already suggested above, but is derived from a different model and so does not dovetail exactly. The 'super-positioning' matrix provides a focus based on organizational values and technical strengths. Once a firm has chosen a position in the matrix it can then proceed to develop a coherent set of 'master' strategies.

Strong delivery	A	B
Strong service	C	D
Strong idea	E	F
	Practice-centred business	Business-centred practice

Fig. 3.11 Possible framework for strategy development

The production of strategies is a creative process and this stage should not be rushed, see Figure 3.12. Initially ridiculous suggestions need to be considered (de Bono, 1971), seeds of thoughts need time to incubate and can lead to other insights. Each firm must generate its own strategies to suit its particular circumstances, personalities and, to an extent, history.

Once the strategies have been developed individually it is important to check that they are mutually supportive and the team will have to work to achieve the greatest collective impact. Success in this respect is crucial to the process, which is, remember, concerned with the firm **as a whole**.

3.4.5 Implementation and review

It is, of course, essential that the strategies are put into effect and to do this it will be necessary to identify individuals within the firm who will be responsible for pursuing matters on a day-to-day level. A mechanism that can assist in this respect is to request that those identified for a given area provide a brief review of that area, say information technology within the firm, and also provide specific targets for the next **12 months**, plus an outline of future actions. In this way the strategies, collectively agreed, become 'owned' at an operational level, and at the same time a control mechanism is instituted as the targets can now be checked and reviewed.

An example of an **annual** business plan from Getz and Stasiowski (1984) is given in Table 3.2.

The review of the strategic plan can therefore be achieved at a detailed level,

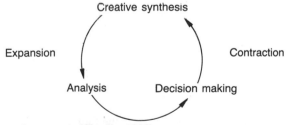

Fig. 3.12 The creative process (Chaplin, 1989)

Table 3.2 Sample outline of annual business plan (Getz and Stasiowski, 1984)

1. Goals and objectives of the organization
List answers to such specific questions as: Where does the firm want to be in five years? How does it expect to get there? What steps in the growth process are to be achieved and by when?

2. Marketing plan
Outline the firm's philosophy on marketing and the organization structure needed to accomplish the marketing plan. Outline tools of the marketing effort and what items need to be produced and expanded. List anticipated project awards by specific marketing areas and dollar amounts. List specific clients wherever possible, amounts expected to be acquired, and estimated dates.

3. Operations plan
List steps to be taken to achieve goals of completing projects on time and within budget. For example, does the firm have a project manager's manual to train new project managers? Outline the procedures to be followed to maximize use of personnel, including sharing of personnel by departments or operating groups. Summarize quality control procedures to be followed. Then develop a monthly forecast of fee income by projecting the balance to be earned on existing contracts and the anticipated earnings on new business acquisitions as outlined in the marketing plan.

4. Financial plan
Based on current backlog, expected new business acquisitions from the marketing plan, and estimated staff capacity, develop a projected income statement and balance sheet for the new year. Develop budgets by operating groups to tie into income statement.

5. Human resources and organization plan
Develop estimates of the number of new employees to be hired based on operating and financial plans, taking into account expected employee attrition. List skills needed and expected levels of compensation. Determine where, how, and when these people will be hired. List any techniques or changes in employee benefit plans that may help the firm retain good people.

6. Administrative support/physical facilities
Outline support staff requirements needed to accomplish business plan. Determine adequacy of present facilities including new space and equipment needs. Determine how and when new equipment is to be purchased or leased. Review list of all lease expiration dates and determine action for those expiring in the plan year as well as for two to three years thereafter.

but the major measures chosen can also be tracked over time to see if the predictions were realistic. As mentioned at the start of this chapter, the strategies should be sufficiently robust that they do not require constant fine-tuning, but if the senior managers lose confidence in the strategic plan then this is the time to start the process again.

3.5 CHECKLIST

Looking long term, say five to ten years into the future:

- Is there a consensus between the managers as to the broad goals they are working towards? Has it ever been discussed?
- Has the firm tracked its own performance over, say, the last five years?
- Has the firm explicitly sought to identify its particular strengths and weaknesses and the major opportunities and threats it faces?
- Does the firm have an agreed and coherent strategy covering its: market position, people, structure, technology and financing?
- Do staff in the firm know where the firm is going?

4 | Marketing

4.1 MARKETING OR SELLING?

Marketing is often confused with 'selling' and both differ considerably from the traditional approach professionals have taken to client relations. In Figure 4.1 a typical progression is suggested with three stages (based on Webb, 1982, p. 27). In **early times** the firm simply **reacts** to clients' demands and provides whatever is required to the best of the firm's ability. This probably was the general pattern in the UK up to about five years ago. For most smaller firms it remains a fair description.

The second stage shown is the **hard sell**, where the firm has developed some standard services for which it then makes efforts to find markets. An example of this would be a firm of surveyors which, in the 1980s, developed a comprehensive package for resolving a whole series of complex technical problems associated with a particular system of housing. The problems involved a dramatic

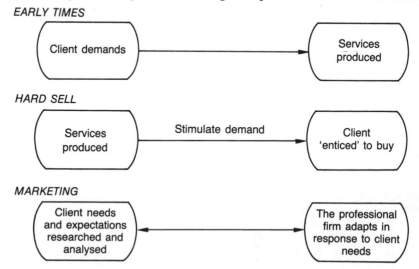

EARLY TIMES

Client demands ⟶ Services produced

HARD SELL

Services produced — Stimulate demand ⟶ Client 'enticed' to buy

MARKETING

Client needs and expectations researched and analysed ⟵ The professional firm adapts in response to client needs

Fig. 4.1 Selling and marketing

fire risk and so, once the firm had perfected its solution, it publicized both the risk and the solution it had developed to all owners of this type of housing. If the firm is engaged in selling then its objective is to achieve a **high volume** of sales in order to maximize its return on the investment made in developing the service in the first instance. This can be a very effective management approach, but it is not marketing.

The third step shown in the diagram is **marketing**, and unlike the previous two alternatives the relationship shown is patently two way. The firm is not merely reacting to demand or endeavouring to stimulate a particular type of demand, it is instead endeavouring to satisfy client needs by working on commissions that it has the abilities and inclination to do particularly well. The aim is to achieve a **fit** between the clients' needs and the firm's needs, both commercial and professional. The key word for marketing is normally given as **client satisfaction**, but it is more accurate to say mutual satisfaction of clients **and** firm.

None of the above approaches is right *per se*. If the firm is successful in the eyes of its partners by just reacting to demand (perhaps it is lucky in the demands made upon it), then what is wrong with that?

It may be that the firm feels it should be more proactive. In a stable business environment – when the firm has established services delivered to a receptive clientele – selling is appropriate, with **efficiency** as the objective. In contrast in a turbulent environment marketing is required, with **effectiveness** as the objective. Many firms feel the need to be more active in their management of client relations and few people would deny that the business environment has for some time been very turbulent. The following sections will therefore consider the marketing approach in more depth.

4.2 KEY FEATURES IN SERVICES MARKETING

The application of marketing principles to professional firms has been blighted by the clumsy translation of principles suitable for manufacturing processes to the professions, which operate in the services sector. The situation has been greatly clarified by the work of the Nordic School of Marketing, with a key contribution from Christian Grönroos. One of the main points of difference that he highlights for services is the fact that production and consumption **overlap**, producing buyer–seller interactions.

4.2.1 Buyer–seller interactions

This is shown in Figure 4.2 (a) and is contrasted with the arrangement for manufacturing (Figure 4.2 (b)). An example of buyer–seller interactions would be when an architect runs a site meeting with the client present. Here the service is being 'produced', but at the same time 'consumed' by the client.

As a result, for services, no hard and fast distinction can be made between the

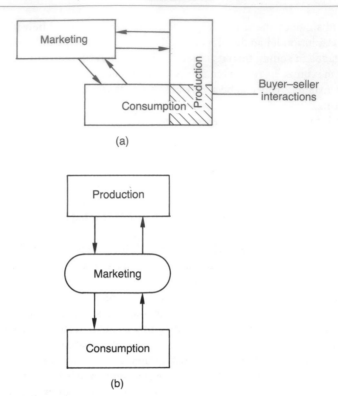

(a)

(b)

Fig. 4.2 Buyer–seller interactions

factory floor where production takes place and the marketing department which sets up a bright and shiny image to the consumers. In the case of a professional firm it is quite possible that the client will come into contact with the great majority of the members of staff of the firm, and in this way it can be said that professional firms are to a great extent **transparent**.

It is common practice for professional firms to make a particular effort with the entrance and reception areas of their offices into which clients are received, and further efforts may be made to the extent of the corridor leading from these areas to a meeting room within which it is hoped the client can be contained. This is an adaptation of the manufacturing approach to marketing and can work reasonably well, but can also result in waves of panic when the client asks for a tour of the offices!

A very positive alternative approach is practised by one leading firm of structural engineers in London. It is quite exceptional, but extraordinary in its simplicity. This firm invites visitors into the centre of its open plan offices to a table where the visitor can sit in comfort and wait, and will subsequently have the meeting. All around members of the firm are working and throughout the offices there are lines and lines of bookshelves meticulously maintained by three full-time librarians. The message of this very simple approach is 'we have nothing to hide'. The clear feeling that a visitor receives is that the firm is good, and knows it is good.

4.2.2 Internal marketing

Once it is appreciated that the client will inevitably see much of the firm, whether by design or by accident, the necessity of **internal** marketing becomes apparent. A key element of marketing is for firms to be outward-looking and sensitive to clients' needs, but managers must not neglect those within the firm in their marketing effort. They should be sensitive to their aspirations and, in addition, endeavour to positively influence the attitudes and **service orientation** of staff so that they confirm and reinforce the image of the firm that is being projected to its clients. One way of stressing the linkage between internal and external marketing is to give pre-eminence to the client–professional relationship and relegate the firm to a facilitating or supporting role, as depicted in Figure 4.3.

One current issue is whether firms should have a marketing department, or at least a partner who concentrates on marketing. Given the implications of buyer–seller interactions, it seems reasonable to suggest an ideal situation in which everyone is part of the marketing effort of the firm. It may be that particular skills at partnership level can be utilized and one person can take the lead in this area, but even in the realms of negotiating for possible contracts it will be necessary for those who have the specialist knowledge to be involved if the firm is to retain its credibility. One thing seems certain, marketing is not something that can be delegated to management specialists, although, of course, inputs from graphic designers and public relations experts can be drawn upon in a supporting role.

4.2.3 Intangibility of services

One of the main difficulties in marketing professional services is that it does not involve a product that can be shown to a potential client so that he or she can say 'Yes, I would like some more of those'. Sibson (1971) puts it well when he says:

The customer of a professional service enterprise is buying confidence.

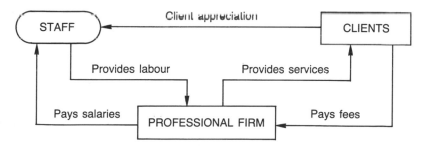

Fig. 4.3 The firm as facilitator

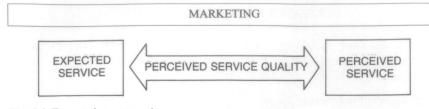

Fig. 4.4 Expectation–perception gap

The implications of this intangibility are far-reaching, especially in terms of the client's assessment of the firm's performance. Given that a key component of effective marketing is client satisfaction, it is self-evident that the way in which the client makes assessments of how well the firm has performed is critical.

4.3 CLIENT'S ASSESSMENT OF SERVICE QUALITY

Again Grönroos has shed light on this area, as shown in Figure 4.4. Unlike manufacturing, where the quality of a product can be measured in tolerances of thousandths of an inch, the assessment of services revolves around the client's **perception** of the service received compared with the client's **expectation** of that service. This process will be elaborated shortly, but at this stage it can be seen that a firm can make efforts in two distinctly different areas – namely, managing the client's initial expectation and managing the client's perception of the service rendered.

4.3.1 Expectation

The client's expectation of the service will be conditioned to a great extent by past experience, but also by the messages used to gain the work in the first instance. There is a distinct danger that in order to obtain the brief the professional may overstate what the firm can deliver, and if this happens the firm will be running to catch up, right from the beginning. It is important to avoid this trap, but the image portrayed must still be positive. For example, if the firm is busy when the client makes initial contact, it can – after expressing genuine interest in the proposition put forward by the client and checking that time is **not** of the essence – take the initiative by saying that it would want time to prepare a reasoned response to the client's request and then go on to make arrangements for a meeting in, say, two weeks' time. In this way the message is conveyed that an in-depth analysis will be provided. It also demonstrates that the firm actively controls its time, and when the meeting is held, and an impressive presentation made, it will also confirm that the firm produces high-quality work, **on time**.

This can be contrasted with a ragged attempt to react immediately, in which case the firm can appear opportunistic and would not provide itself sufficient time to make a professional presentation at the first meeting with the client.

4.3.2 Perception

The second area where effort can be directed is at the client's perception of the service rendered. It is important to stress that there is never any objective measurement of a professional service; it will always depend on individual assessments, which in turn will be based on multiple impressions from a variety of sources. It is, perhaps, easiest to highlight the problem by looking at one extreme situation: the job where everything goes right!

In this case the **objective** quality of the service provided is clearly high; however, it is quite possible that the client will be unaware of the firm's efforts simply because nothing has gone wrong. Doubtless the firm will have given due weight to the well-known aphorism 'a stitch in time saves nine', that is, they will have foreseen potential difficulties and taken action early so that matters do not get out of control. Quite simply, they have avoided problems. As a result, the part played by the professional firm will appear deceptively simple. A cynical view would suggest that the firm would be better advised to let things go awry, to an extent, and then they could take decisive and visible action to ensure that, let's say, the **contractor** puts right the defective work. The client will be duly impressed and give credit to the professional firm.

Unfortunately there is a grain of truth in the above suggestion, but of course there is nothing **professional** about it. The initial problem remains that if the firm does a very good job, the client may very well not realize. A positive reaction to this is for the firm to keep the client informed of potential dangers and the steps being taken so that it is clear that the input of the firm is positive, is proactive and is **working**. This approach involves taking the client through the job with you, rather than just handing over the final product. It is important not to take too heavy-handed an approach to this and it would probably be inadvisable to avail the client with a copy of all correspondence unless this has been particularly requested. Ensuring that the client is involved need only take occasional phone calls, invitations to meetings, etc., and, in addition to demonstrating the attention to detail of the firm, it can also have very beneficial spin-offs in terms of effective brief development.

4.3.3 Technical and functional quality

Figure 4.5 is based on Grönroos's full diagram and builds on Figure 4.4, but includes information on how the judgement between expectation and perception is conditioned. Grönroos suggests two main categories of factors which together build up the corporate image of the firm, which in turn provides the main input to the client's assessment of the service provided.

The two areas referred to break down into **technical quality** and **functional quality**. Technical quality is concerned with **what** is done and it is the area with which professionals, generally speaking, would be mainly interested. It includes how well the problems were solved and the systems and techniques used. It is important to appreciate that clients may assess even technical quality in what may,

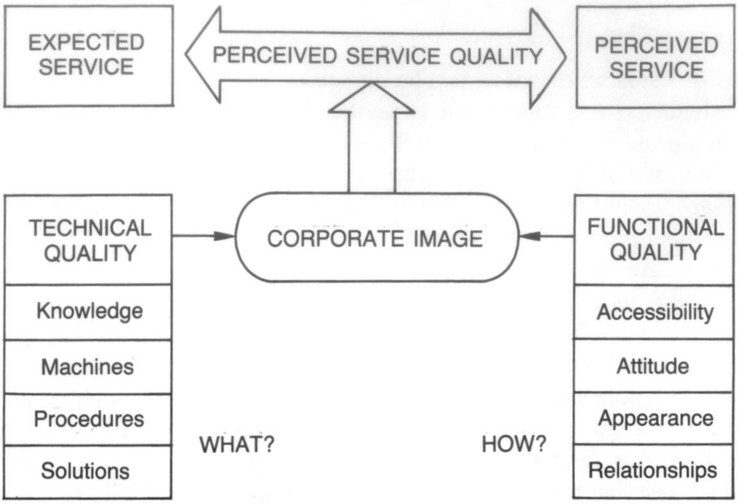

Fig. 4.5 Technical and functional quality

to the professional, appear a rather maverick way.

For example, one firm of architects had done work for a good client, who had provided repeat business over a number years, until suddenly the commissions dried up. As far as the architects were concerned they had made no mistakes and the contact at the client had made no comment. Eventually the firm employed a 'researcher' to talk to the client very sensitively in order to discover what was wrong. The contact at the client was slightly embarrassed and said it was not really anything important enough to mention – but the doorknobs to the boardroom, which the architects had refurbished, kept falling off! The message is clear. Lines of communication must be established and meticulously maintained to ensure that high-quality feedback is received.

The functional factors are even less likely to spring immediately to mind, and revolve around **how** the service was rendered. They include items like the appearance of staff, their attitude towards clients and how accessible the firm's staff were to the client. There is a growing body of research which indicates that when clients judge the quality of a service, they give unexpectedly high weightings to the functional factors compared with the technical factors. Thus, it is important for professionals to think through **how** they deal with their clients as an important, and quite separate, issue from **what** they do to solve the technical problems they are faced with.

4.3.4 Image formation

A central part of the diagram is the image of the firm, and a complementary way of looking at this particular aspect is shown in Figure 4.6. This reinforces the suggestion that images are the result of multiple impressions, and in this case the

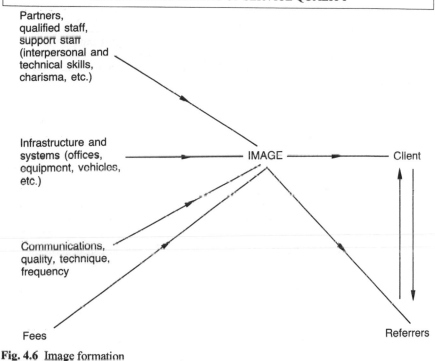

Fig. 4.6 Image formation

division is not made between technical and functional factors but rather people, 'things', communications and fees. Each of these groupings contributes to the image of the firm and in each case it is a matter of providing an appropriate message.

Clearly, the people involved in the firm must look the part, and if they dress like beggars they cannot expect to be trusted with controlling, or spending, the client's money. But the image provided by people of the firm can be reinforced, or confused, by the offices, equipment and vehicles they use. It is quite common for firms in cities like London to run different offices for different market sectors, with relatively ostentatious offices for commercial clients and more modest offices for public sector work.

Everything the firm does conveys a message, and it can be very embarrassing to attend a cost-cutting exercise at a small housing refurbishment job when the partner's car is worth several times the cost of the heating installation it has been necessary to exclude from the contract. Sensitivity is required. Similarly with communications, where messages are conveyed by the headed notepaper used, etc., but more importantly the reliability with which messages are taken and calls returned. It is common currency that the client's first contact with the firm is often through the receptionist, and the impression given at this point is crucial. The last area highlighted is that of fees, and here the problem is to judge the level of fees charged in order to strike a balance between inferring that the firm is an inferior

Table 4.1 Example questionnaire for client satisfaction (Wilson, A, 1984.)

Thank you for using our services. We appreciate very much your trust and confidence. We are interested in improving them. We would appreciate your assisting us by completing this questionnaire and returning it in the stamped, self-addressed envelope. Your response will be kept confidential.

YES / NO

——— ——— 1. Did you feel our office personnel were friendly and treated you courteously?

——— ——— 2. Why did you select our practice originally? . . . .
. . . .

——— ——— 3. Did our office keep you adequately informed regarding your project? If not, do you have any suggestions on how we might improve on this? . . . .
. . . .

——— ——— 4. Did you feel the surveyor working on your project spent sufficient time with you?

——— ——— 5. Did you feel that sufficient attention and care was devoted to your project?

——— ——— 6. Were your telephone enquiries answered to you satisfaction?

——— ——— 7. Were you kept adequately informed of progress?

——— ——— 8. Do you feel that our fee for services was reasonable for the work we performed?

——— ——— 9. We would appreciate any comments that you might have that will help us to improve our services to our clients. Please use the reverse side of this sheet if necessary.

Thank you very much for your time and courtesy in filling out this questionnaire.

good (in economic terms) and giving the impression that the firm expects to be paid a lot of money for a relatively simple job.

An important point to note, which transcends the individual factors, is that the firm should, as far as possible, ensure that the messages provided by the various aspects confirm and reinforce each other rather than give a confusing or disjointed image.

Given the importance of the client's level of satisfaction with the firm, it clearly makes sense for the firm to make positive efforts to discover the client's view on the various aspects of the service provided. If the firm works alongside the client, as already suggested above, a lot of feedback can be gained day-to-day, especially if staff are tutored into habitually, but sensitively, seeking the views of clients' representatives. Firms can employ independent third parties, as shown in the example above involving the boardroom doorknobs. Another alternative is the use of client questionnaires to obtain a reflective assessment of how well the firm is satisfying the client's needs. An example is given in Table 4.1.

4.3.5 Referrers

Figure 4.6 includes an additional element which has not been mentioned before, that is the group of people termed **referrers**. The image created is obviously received by the clients of the firm direct, but it also reaches third parties who may not themselves employ the firm, but who **do** relay the image, possibly in a distorted way, to people who then become clients of the firm. The situation shown in the diagram is relatively simple, but in fact the message could pass via several referrers before it has reached the potential client.

How this particular part of the image formation system works is not fully understood at present, although it is generally held to be a very important source of instruction, especially when it is appreciated that current clients also act as particularly well-informed referrers. For instance, a recent report (RICS, 1991) found that 53% of new instructions for building surveying practices originated from referrers, see Figure 4.7. Many practitioners put this percentage higher.

Research is currently under way (Barrett and Hoxley, 1992) to illuminate how the referral system operates in practice and initial findings based on a case study indicate that for one firm in a provincial town, which has now started tracking referrals by simply asking new clients where they heard of the firm, there are only four major sources of referral within the town and that positive actions towards these individuals (something as simple as a letter saying 'thank you') has resulted in an even higher level of instruction from these sources. It is quite possible, in fact, that firms could best direct their efforts at referrers in that these key people may be less numerous than potential clients and more influential in such clients' decision-making processes than the firm itself can be.

4.4 EXPANDING THE FIRM'S WORKLOAD

In order to survive firms need to do well the work they obtain in order to build their reputations. As a result, the time that can be devoted to actively expanding the

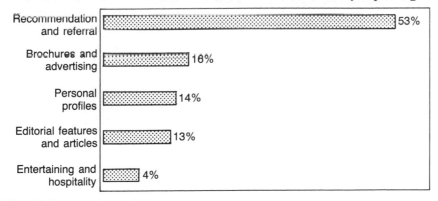

Fig. 4.7 Sources of commissions

workload is limited and it is thus important that the efforts that are made should be focused in areas where success is most likely.

4.4.1 Service/market matrix

Figure 4.8 shows the service/market matrix (Wilson, A., 1984, p. 77) with existing services and new services along the top and existing clients and new clients down the side. This creates four sectors. A note of which of the firm's resources are being used in each situation is given in each body of the table. The actual composition of the table itself is important in that it treats not only the **services** that have been developed by the firm as a resource that it has to offer, but it also stresses that the firm's **client base** is a second resource that the firm can positively use.

Cell 1 is characterized by the firm's work which is based on existing services provided to existing clients. It is here that some of the simplest ways to build the firm's workload can be overlooked. Cross-selling existing services to existing clients who do not at present use that service merely puts together the two resource bases the firm has in different configurations. A client for whom the firm controlled building projects may also be interested in fire valuations of their property stock, or tax advice on their property investments. Actions are therefore required to inform clients of the full range of services available from the firm and this, backed up by tactful research, may reveal great potential to expand activities.

Maister (1989) highlights one of the problems with activities in cell 1, and this is the fact that it is perhaps less exciting for the professionals involved and, in addition, firms often operate a differential reward system weighted in favour of new clients as opposed to extra work from existing clients. This is perhaps unwittingly done and can fairly easily be exposed by reference to the income data the firm holds. Maybe it is right to break open the champagne when a new client is gained by the practice, but if new commissions from existing clients are not similarly welcomed, the partners should not be surprised if less effort is made in this direction, probably with unanticipated consequences.

Cells 2 and 3 of the matrix show 'related diversifications', where the firm builds on an existing resource but has to add a new element. In the case of cell 2 this

	Existing services	New services
Existing clients	1 Existing capabilities facilities and clients	3 Client resource. No existing capability or facility resource
New clients	2 Existing capability and facilities. No client resource	4 Nil

Fig. 4.8 Service/market matrix

Table 4.2 Possible descriptors for profiling exercise (Wilson, A., 1984, p. 36-8)

This list is based on commercial client characteristics but many of the factors for consideration can be applied either unadjusted or slightly adjusted for private clients.

1. Size of client by any or all of the following
   —turnover
   —profit
   —assets employed
   —numbers employed
   —number of establishments
   —size of establishments
   —ROI
   —other

2. Form of organizations
   —owner managed
   —limited company
   —international/multinational/local/regional/national
   —extent of verticalization
   —cooperative
   —voluntary purchasing group
   —franchise
   —other

3. Extent of specialization (distributors)
   —full line
   —associated products
   —complementary products
   —general suppliers

4. Type of outlet (distributors)
   —retailer
   —wholesaler
   —cash-and-carry
   —merchants
   —stockholder
   —agent
   —dealer (franchised and others)
   —rack jobber
   —voluntary group
   —discount
   —mail order

involves new clients for services the firm already provides. Where firms have tightly packaged services, such as a fully worked through system for refurbishing a very specific type of dwelling, then they are engaged in 'selling' with the objective of achieving high volume sales in order to recoup their investment in developing the service, preferably plus interest!

Viewing the development of the firm's client base in a broader context, Wilson, A. (1984, pp. 134–5) has suggested an approach he terms **profiling**. This involves the use of internal cost and time data about existing clients and projects. By analysis of these data the firm can identify a set of descriptors of those types of clients with whom the firm has particularly beneficial dealings. The descriptors should be as simple as possible and examples drawn from Wilson's text are included in Table 4.2. By then **positively** seeking additional clients that fit the identified profile, the chances are greatly enhanced of gaining more work, satisfying the new clients and meeting the firm's objectives. In this way the firm can focus its efforts in directions that are likely to be fruitful.

The other related diversification, into cell 3, involves the development of new services to satisfy the requirements of the firm's existing client base. A prerequisite of an expansion in this direction is, of course, to identify the client's unsatiated need, and this is best achieved through informal discussion and an attitude that is receptive to information from a wide variety of sources. Once identified the challenge is then to develop the new service, and in conceptual terms this simply means finding ways through which the firm can acquire the knowledge required.

Such knowledge can be introduced through the employment of staff with the necessary specialist skills; it can be developed in-house through research by staff; or this research could in fact be subcontracted to academics; lastly, the firm can acquire the knowledge required through collaborative arrangements with other firms. In this last case the firm is truly treating its client base as a resource that can give it a strong negotiating position *vis-à-vis* other firms who may have the necessary specialist technical knowledge, but not a well-maintained relationship with an appropriate client. For example, at one time government grants were available for improving the energy efficiency of heating boilers in hotels. A firm of surveyors, with a number of clients from this market sector, linked with heating and ventilating engineers with specialist knowledge to provide a very attractive service to a number of proprietors, who were thus able to gain the benefit of the government grant.

The choice of mechanism to acquire the necessary knowledge would depend on many factors, but a major consideration will be the likely volume and reliability of the demand in the longer term. If there is likely to be a lot of work over an extended period, then it is sensible for the firm to invest in research or the employment of specialist staff.

The last sector of Figure 4.8, cell 4, differs from all the others in that the firm has neither a client nor a technical resource and it is self-evident that to move into work where this description applies is a high-risk exercise. It would be like a firm of quantity surveyors experienced in cost control of public sector housing seeking and taking on the design input for commercial new build projects. If the firm can see that great benefits can be obtained from gaining work in an area that comes within cell 4, then rather than leaping across to an unrelated diversification, a much safer route would be via cells 2 or 3 – that is, first extend the client base and then develop the technology, or *vice versa*. In this way the risk element is at least contained to an extent.

So, it can be seen that by viewing the experience of the firm and its clients as two different types of resources various opportunities to build on existing success can be identified. In addition, ways of reducing risk have been suggested so that limited resources can be deployed to greatest effect.

4.4.2 A market distribution view

Remembering that in endeavouring to expand the firm's workload efforts must be made to maximize the impact of what will necessarily be limited efforts, it is possible to view the problem in terms of competing firms. This is illustrated in Figure 4.9.

The point made in the diagram is that it is quite feasible, certainly within a locality, for a firm to identify its main competitors and to categorize them by size and specialization. There is likely to be a broad relationship between small specialist firms working in high-fee areas and large generalist firms working at lower margins. It may very well not be this simple in practice, but the key to the approach is to plot the firms graphically and identify any gaps. If the subject firm can then position itself in a gap, the probability of competing successfully is enhanced due to the differentiation of image and services offered that can be developed. An extreme example of this occurred a few years ago when a group of three very eminent men, all from different parts of the construction industry, set up in practice to deal, as experts, in high-value construction disputes. They typified the small, highly specialized, high-fee type of firm. They had a very distinctive image and thus created a market niche within which to operate.

Maister's typology of firms, already mentioned in Chapter 2, links with the above ideas and is shown diagrammatically in Figure 4.10. Firms do have a choice how big to be and this section stresses that that choice should be explicit, based on

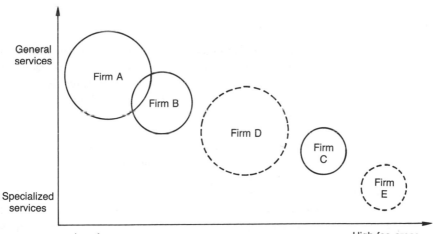

Fig. 4.9 Market positioning of firm

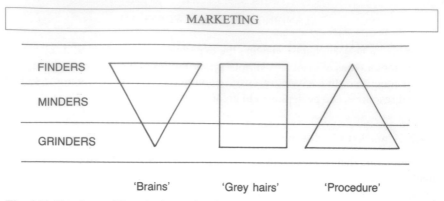

FINDERS

MINDERS

GRINDERS

'Brains'   'Grey hairs'   'Procedure'

Fig. 4.10 Typology of firms in the marketplace

an informed view of the business environment and, of course, the objectives of those who make up the firm.

Now that various features of marketing have been discussed we shall turn to a simple process view of gaining instructions and the practical actions open to a firm at each step.

4.5 PROCESS VIEW OF MARKETING

Assuming that the firm has identified the client groupings with which it wants to make contact, there are three levels at which actions can be taken: general, indirect and direct. Once contact has been made there remains the issue of how to demonstrate the firm's suitability.

4.5.1 Making contact

(a) *General*

Efforts at the general level are simply intended to raise awareness of the firm in the public eye, or maybe within a particular sector of the public. The work of professional institutions comes into this category and to a large extent is designed to explain what their members do and how it can be of use. Groupings of firms within a given geographical area may also band together for a similar purpose. For example, many branches of the Royal Institution of Chartered Surveyors Building Surveyors' Division, a type of surveyor that is not widely known, have jointly issued explanatory brochures about building surveying which has been given to all libraries, solicitors and others who come into contact with potential clients. The brochures include a list of all of the firms on the back cover.

Another way in which the public relations message can be reinforced is through consistency of design for notepaper, etc., used by firms and in this connection the use of institutional logos on the stationery of member firms is a good example, see Figure 4.11.

Fig. 4.11 Example of institution's 'logo'

Thus, at a general level the thrust is to raise awareness of the services available, benefits that can be obtained and to provide easy recognition of those who can provide the services. Action can also be taken to associate the professional firm with high-profile activities which provide reflected glory such as charity work, informed comment at government level, etc.

(b) *Indirect*

Efforts at the general level are important but are unlikely to result in specific instructions for individual firms, with the possible exception of the shared brochure. Until the last five to ten years, if a firm wanted to pursue work positively, the best it could do, owing to restrictive by-laws, was to use an indirect approach. This stopped short of directly approaching clients and instead endeavoured to create situations in which the conditions are favourable for client contact to occur.

For instance, many firms have developed expertise in particular areas and have then encouraged their in-house 'expert' to write articles or speak at seminars and conferences and, in so doing, raised the general status of the firm and gave the opportunity for potential clients to discover what the firm has to offer and approach the expert, thus making that initial contact. The danger to avoid with this approach is to inadvertently spend a lot of time speaking to your fellow professionals rather than to potential clients or influential referrers. Articles should be placed, not in learned journals, but in *Financial Times* or whatever your clients read! Likewise with seminars and conferences.

Membership of clubs, associations and work on the committees of professional institutions can all serve a similar purpose to the above approach, in that a network of contacts is developed so that messages can be quickly and efficiently relayed about potential work to those who would like to do it.

There were other ways in which the 'hands off' approach dictated by the by-laws could, to a certain extent, be circumvented. By approaching a client through a third party who already knew and worked with that client, or through the astute use of market intelligence. A good example of the latter was when the senior partner of a firm managed to arrange to be on the same train as a major client for a four-hour journey. They, of course, just happened to bump into each other!

Over recent years the by-laws of the professional institutions have been relaxed so that direct approaches can be made to potential clients although this is usually subject to some restrictions to avoid acrimonious competition between individual firms and, in general, behaviour unbefitting professionals.

Although firms generally do not **have** to rely on indirect approaches, these techniques should not be discarded. They can be very effective at carrying a strong but subtle message about the professional standing of the firm. This is hard to quantify, but is a powerful marketing lever.

(c) *Direct*

A key step in making direct approaches is to identify the right individual in the client body. For example, one firm went through a complete negotiation with an individual, and employed extra staff for the project, only to discover that the person they had been dealing with did not have the authority to grant the contract, and in the end the firm did not get the work. Background research is necessary and the general objective is to gain a full understanding of how the client organization operates and the roles of the various people within that organization. Once the client's system is understood then actions can be taken against this background. A very well-known model of the type of arrangement that could exist within the client system (Bonoma, 1982), adapted for the professional situation by Wilson, A. (1984, p. 95), is given in Figure 4.12. One person may perform all the roles, but when dealing with institutional clients there is likely to be some separation of duties. The firm must be alive to this possibility and work in such a way that it interacts with the client systems it faces effectively, in each case.

4.5.2 Demonstrating suitability

So far various approaches to reaching potential clients have been discussed. Once

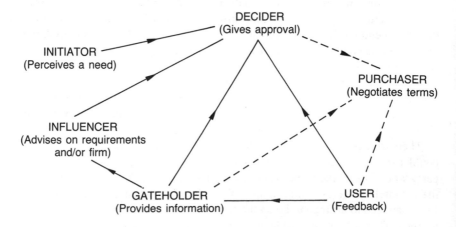

Fig. 4.12 Possible client 'buying' system

contact has been made it is then necessary to demonstrate the firm's suitability to the client. This may involve a request to send information about the practice or, in fact, a presentation by the firm may be requested.

Whichever medium is being used it is essential that the firm stresses the **benefits** it can provide for the client rather than dwelling too much on the **features** of its particular approach. This may sound obvious, but it is easy for professionals to be absorbed in the details of what they do, which may be impressive in some ways, but unless the client can see a benefit from those skills it is unlikely that the firm will obtain the commission. It is therefore necessary for those involved from the professional firm to step outside their own particular interests and to endeavour to gain an objective understanding of the client's organization, its needs and the ways in which their firm can satisfy those needs.

Taking the above approach, if **written material** is requested it should be designed and chosen to demonstrate how the firm has solved similar problems for other clients, rather than just presenting a historical review of all past projects. The image created should be consistent, but tailored to the characteristics of particular clients. It is undoubtedly better to produce a simple, but well-designed single sheet than a rambling, poorly presented ten-page brochure. If there is no perceived client demand for publicity material, then the firm should not feel guilty if it does not have a 'glossy brochure'. For most firms, however, it can be a useful tool if it is well designed and used sensitively.

It may be that the potential client requests a **presentation** and, indeed, this is becoming increasingly common for the construction professions, particularly, of course, for those dealing with corporate clients. It is essential that those involved in presentations prepare well and rehearse their input, including a dry run. The first part of the presentation should endeavour to build a relationship with the audience (Coxe, 1983) and in this sense an oral presentation is much better than a video, which does not allow easy interaction between those involved. The presentation should demonstrate a problem-solving approach which is interpreted in terms of the client's needs. The scope of the presentation should be limited to the main points of interest to the client – that is, not necessarily technicalities, but probably time and money!

It is essential that the allotted time is not exceeded and the presentation should be so designed that the firm leaves behind one major point which reinforces the firm's suitability for the commission and differentiates it from the other competing firms. For instance, it might be that the firm has specialist expertise in the area or is one of the few firms of sufficient size to handle a project of the magnitude involved. If a firm can develop effective skills at presentations, they can be a powerful source of work.

4.5.3 Communication

For written and verbal approaches the basic tenets of communications theory should be observed (e.g. Adair, 1973). This is a large topic, but the main points are:

- The message should be **reinforced**, that is previewed, stated and then summarized. In addition, verbal and visual images created should compound positively.
- The message should be **coded** into a language that the 'audience' will understand. This may well include the rephrasing of technical terms that could cause confusion. The message should be free of ambiguous and value-laden words which can have an unpredictable impact.
- An effort should be made to obtain **feedback**. When sending written material this can be a request for the client's reaction to the information provided or follow-up telephone call. In a presentation, the ideal is to generate productive debate, but if this is not possible then non-verbal signals should be observed (see Table 4.3 for examples).

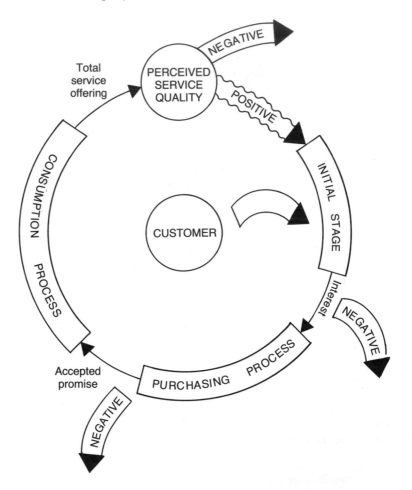

Fig. 4.13 Stages in the client–professional relationship (Grönroos, 1984)

Table 4.3 Non-verbal cues (Burstein and Stasiowski, 1982)

Defensiveness	Arms crossed on chest
	Legs over chair arm while seated
	Sitting in armless chair reversed
	Crossing legs
	Fistlike gestures
	Pointing index finger
	Karate chops
Suspicion	Not looking at you
	Arms crossed
	Moving away from you
	Silhouette body towards you
	Sideways glance
	Feet/body pointing towards exit
	Touching/rubbing nose
	Rubbing eyes
	Buttoning coat – drawing away
Readiness	Hands on hips
	Hands on mid-thigh when seated
	Sitting on edge of chair
	Arms spread gripping edge of table/desk
	Moving closer
	Sprinter's position
Cooperation	Sprinter's position
	Open hands
	Sitting on edge of chair
	Hand-to-face gestures
	Unbuttoning coat
	Tilted head

Territorial dominance	Feet on desk
	Feet on chair
	Leaning against/touching object
	Placing object in a desired space
	Elevating oneself
	Cigar smokers
	Hands behind head – leaning back
Nervousness	Clearing throat
	'Whew' sound
	Whistling
	Cigarette smoking
	Picking/pinching flesh
	Fidgeting in chair
	Hands covering mouth while speaking
	Not looking at the other person
	Tugging at parts while seated
	Jingling money in pockets
	Tugging at ear
	Perspiration/wringing of hands
Boredom	Doodling
	Drumming
	Legs crossed – foot kicking
	Head in palm of hand(s)
	Blank stare
	Bored stiff

4.6 CONCLUSION

The above discussion gets us to the point where, hopefully, a new commission comes to the firm. It is important to remember that this is the beginning of a relationship with a new client and the best way to obtain work is through the high reputation of the firm. It is therefore essential that each client's job is done well. This can then open up possibilities for further work, either repeat business or cross-selling within the existing client base of the firm, or indeed work obtained via referrals from existing clients or others with a knowledge of the firm. Figure 4.13 summarizes the various stages in the client–professional relationship and brings this chapter full circle.

4.7 CHECKLIST

- Does the firm actively get feedback from its clients on its performance?
- Does the firm really balance the expectations set up to gain work with the service it can realistically deliver?
- Does the firm make efforts to keep the client informed as to what it is doing for the client, even when there are no problems?
- Has the firm really considered the implications of being transparent to the client?
- Are all members of the firm encouraged to become client-oriented in how they provide the service?
- Has the firm a clear view of its market position? Is it occupying a specialist niche or is it in the mainstream? Does this position make sense given the level of expertise of its staff?
- Does the firm find out where new clients heard of the firm? Does it make efforts to build good relationships with its principal referrers?
- When making presentations to clients, do you focus on the **benefits** of the proposals for your client?

Cost and time control

5

5.1 GENERALLY

To a great extent cost and time within the professional firm can be viewed interchangeably in that the time spent by staff is the major cost. The extent to which firms allow staff further down the hierarchy to be aware of budgets, etc., varies considerably. Some firms make a distinction between junior staff and partners, with the former only seeing the data in terms of time, whereas they are converted to financial figures at partnership level where obviously all the costs, such as accommodation, stationery, etc., have to be included.

Cost and time control can impinge on various facets of a firm's operations. It can be used to support strategic management and marketing decisions, as a basis for dividing profits between the partners, to support the assessment of staff, or to control individual projects. It should be clear from the above list – in particular the last suggestion, project control – that the function involved cannot be satisfied by the firm's formal accounts which are prepared in arrears for a given year, and probably not fully audited for several months, if not years, even then. The system required for cost and time control within the firm must be much more responsive and operate as closely as possible to 'real time'.

5.2 CONTROL MODEL

The basic building block for control is the feedback loop. A familiar example is given in Figure 5.1, involving the heating unit for a building and its thermostat. If the thermostat has not been properly set, or cannot detect that the temperature has gone outside the desirable range, or if it is defective and cannot switch the boiler on or off, then there is no effective control. In general terms, for **effective** control it is necessary to:

- establish standards
- obtain information on deviations from those standards
- have the power to remedy any deviations detected.

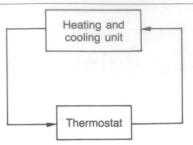

Fig. 5.1 A simple feedback control system

If any of these three elements is missing then effective control is impossible (Donelly *et al.*, 1981).

The three factors will now be considered in turn, but specifically applied to cost and time control within the professional firm.

5.2.1 Establishing standards

The key step that a firm must take if it is to institute effective cost and time control is very simple: it must predict its fee income and in this way create budgets against which actual performance can be checked.

This is almost invariably done on a project basis unless there are categories of work involving many minor items that can be better grouped together. Analysis with the project approach then hinges on the job number given to each project as the instruction is received. Figure 5.2 shows a very basic, but perfectly adequate, fee forecast.

The first column shows the project title, after which the job number appears. The next three columns show the calculation of total fees anticipated for each project. The following column shows fees charged to date and the last column, in the left hand block, gives a descriptive check on work done so far. After this the remainder of the table is set out as a calendar across which the fee stage payments are ranged. By totalling the figures vertically, the expected income on a monthly basis can be identified and checked with actual fees invoiced.

It is possible to analyse the information in order to produce a further control measure, that is, the firm's 'backlog period'. This is shown schematically in Figure 5.3, slightly elaborated by the categorization of work into 'certain' and 'possible'. The backlog period will vary from firm to firm. For instance, a firm that does predominantly structural surveys could have a backlog period of only two weeks (unlikely, but possible), whereas a firm working on a major, phased, science park could look forward to a known workload for five or ten years ahead. It is important that the firm gets a feel for its own typical backlog period and, by monitoring this measure, possible problems can be spotted well in advance.

The above, though very simple, captures the essence of the process. It can, of course, be very much more sophisticated (e.g. Head and Head, 1988).

The simple example given in the Table 5.1 assumes that an *ad valorem* fee is

| JOB | JOB No. | FEES | | | FEES REC'D TO DATE | STAGE AT 1st ___ | JAN. | FEB. | MAR. | APRIL | MAY | JUNE | JULY | AUG. | SEPT. | OCT. | NOV. | DEC. |
		COST	%	TOTAL														
House Millmead	9201	18,000	10	1800	1400	Services in		200		200								
Imps & Reps. 45 Chatham St.	9202	7,000	12½	875	—	Sketches app'd		400		300		175						
Warehouse 'Peterboro'	9203	60,000	6	3,600	2,000	jetting out	400		800		400		400					
Imps & Reps. Bedford	9204	10,000	5	500	—	Sketches		200		300								
Survey Banbury	9205	Time costs		150	—	not started		150										
Offices Glasgow	9206	100,000	6	6000	1000	drawings complete	3000		1000			1000						
House Convers. Bristol	9207	50,000	10	5000	3000	onsite	250	250	260	250	1000							
Shops-Imps Leeds	9208	20,000	3	600	—	not started						200		400				
Shops-Imps Wakefield	9209	15,000	3	450	—	not started							200	250				
etc.																		
TOTAL EXPECTED EACH MONTH																		
CUM. TOTAL																		
INVOICED																		

Fig. 5.2 Example approach to fee forecasts

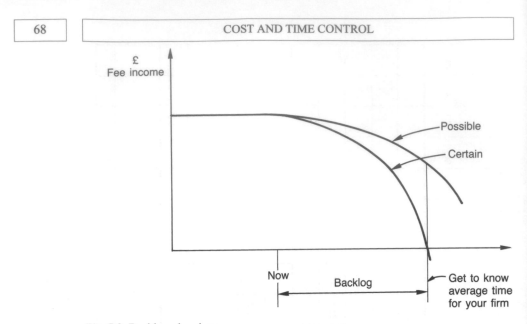

Fig. 5.3 Backlog planning

being used, that is, a percentage fee has simply been applied to the contract sum. Given the ever-increasing incidence of fee tendering it is likely, and in any event desirable, that the firm should analyse the personnel who will be working on the project, or at least the level of seniority of the staff to be involved, and how long they will be spending on it. This link with the known cost of staff to the firm will allow costs as well as income to be predicted. The following section looks at monitoring progress in terms of costs. Later in the chapter the issue of income is considered.

5.2.2 Information on actual progress

Focusing on the firm's costs, there are three areas to monitor: staff time, overheads and disbursements. Information on staff time is collected on time sheets, an example of which is given in Figure 5.4. Staff time expended is allocated against individual job numbers which, when totalled for all staff, allows the total time on given projects to be checked.

In addition to time, the format shown includes a work stages facility, so that important project thresholds can also be monitored. When the code changes a new stage has been started. This may have implications, for instance, for submitting an interim fee account. It can also be used to check against anticipated progress.

The bottom part of the table is for non-fee-earning time so that it can still be controlled to an extent. Maister (1982, p. 19) suggests, for example, that for senior members of the firm 'target utilization' might be around 75%, while more junior staff are likely to spend 90% of their time on fee-earning tasks. By recording how

Time Sheet

1 Complete where arrow shown, thus ►
2 Complete to nearest **actual** half-hour (show as decimal 0.5)
3 Use separate line for each 0 on same job
4 0 = Modified Work Stage Codes; see on right
5 For holidays + leave 1 day to be shown as 7 hours

Modified Work Stage Codes (0):

A Initial Appraisal/Feasibility (Stages A+B)
C Scheme Design (Stages C+D)
E Working Drawing/Spec/BQ (Stages E+F+G)
H Tender action/Site operations/Final a/c (Stages H–L)
T Consultancy + reports etc. to be charged on time basis
U Professional work (Party Wall/Dilapidations, etc.)

Surname ► A. JONES

Office use only:
Month + Year ► OCTOBER 19 94

Abbreviated Job Title	Job No.	Hours
MANOR GDNS	6076 H	29½
N.H.H.T	22	16
NORTON FOLGATE	6986 A	13
	42	4
P.C.HA	21	20½
New Bond St.	7000 A	10½
	62	2½
51/52 HANS.PL.	6741 E	6½
R.B.KINGSTON	2	4
OLDHAM ESTATE		3
		4
H CITY RD	3	17
22 CARLISLE ST	A	8
L.E CAMDEN		3
NORTON FOLGATE	6986 C	27

Sub-Total ► 168½

	Hours
01 Paid Holidays	7
02 Education/CPD/Study Leave	
03 Public Holidays	
04 Management	
05 Special Leave of Absence	
06 Institution Committees	
07 PR – Marketing	
08 Sickness	7
09	
10	

Total ► 182½

Partner's
Initials +
Date

Fig. 5.4 Example time sheet

time is spent, by building a picture of the firm's norms and by monitoring activities, the firm can control the overall magnitude of non-fee-earning time for various levels of staff and, if desired, the balance of activities that make up this fairly large part of the firm's potential resources.

For disbursements, individual job records are kept and travelling, printing and any other direct costs are recorded and periodically summarized against the job numbers. Overheads are typically included in the charging rate for staff time. Overheads include expenses for accommodation, firm's cars, stationery, etc., and for those members of staff who are not closely related to specific projects, principally secretaries. The cost for all these items is therefore added to the hourly rate used to cost project-related staff time inputs.

The above procedures allow cost control to be exercised, but their power is much enhanced if, instead of the projects being cost centres, they are converted to **profit centres**. Figure 5.5 shows how this is achieved in principle, with cost data such as time sheets being collated and then combined with income data to give a measure of profitability per project. If this is done in ratio terms – that is, taking the profit as a percentage margin of income – then comparisons can be made between projects. Also, by collecting projects together in different ways very useful aggregate information can be extracted about project managers and their groupings within the firm, about different clients and about different worktypes.

This may sound obvious, but many firms keep data either at the level of individual projects or in global terms – that is, for the firm as a whole. Because there is no intermediate aggregation the opportunity is lost to provide decision

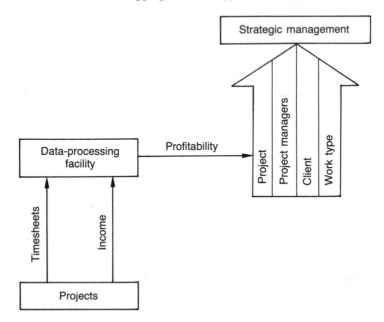

Fig. 5.5 Creating profit centres

support information for the areas mentioned before, namely: strategic management, marketing, allocation of profit and staff/team management.

For example, it was not until one firm instituted fairly strict cost and time control systems and aggregated the data by client, did they realize that one client they had worked for, for over fifteen years, had in fact been consistently loss making. The issue of dividing profit between partners can be a contentious one, especially as cost and time control systems operate in a short time scale and so may not allow sufficient credit for past work brought in, or in fact for development work done to support the firm's future.

This aggregate information should be presented as summary management reports so that broad problem areas can be identified and then a detailed search focused on the problem area only. In this way, by using what in systems theory are called **cones of resolution**, managers' time and efforts can be used to greatest effect. The approach is shown diagrammatically in Figure 5.6 (Schoderbek *et al.*, 1980, p. 291).

Care must be taken in instituting reward mechanisms as they can distort the proper operation of the firm. For instance, if partners are rewarded against those jobs they control, they may try to gain and retain control of a lucrative new job even if it is not within the specialism of their particular department. This may be overcome by making their rewards more dependent on the firm's overall performance. In the area of assessing staff it is also very easy to create tensions if **individuals** are being assessed, and it is probably better to keep the assessment at team level if the firm needs people to work together.

When controlling the projects, the key factor is to have timely systems so that, in addition to having their relevant data, it is not too late to take remedial action. This last point links with the next section.

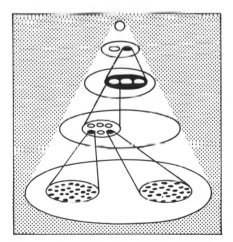

Cones of resolution. Each distinguishable feature at one level may represent a wealth of detail when examined on a larger scale.

Fig. 5.6 Cones of resolution approach

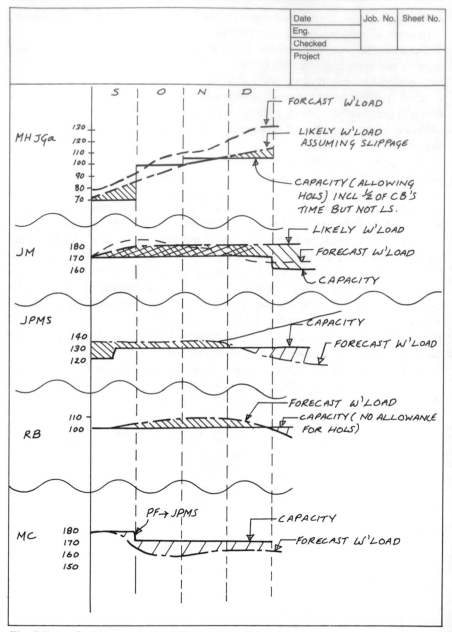

Fig. 5.7 A refreshing approach to manpower planning

5.2.3 Ability to remedy deviations

If hands-on control is required rather than just retrospective data, then it is necessary to include specific features, such as the work stages mentioned above, which then

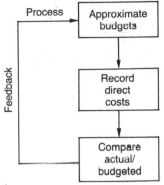

Fig. 5.8 Cost and time control process

enable progress to be monitored. The problem of getting sufficiently quick feed-back has been largely overcome by computerization. In many offices now any member of staff can log in to the details of a project and can see the costs incurred against the project compared with forecasts. Alternatively, it may be that the firm can achieve the desired level of control just as effectively with less sophistication. The example, given in Figure 5.7 shows the approach taken by what must be one of the country's best managed, and quite large, firms of structural engineers.

5.2.4 The process summarized

There are three main stages, as shown in Figure 5.8. Typically in the past the process would have been assessed monthly, but now the comparisons and feedback can occur at any time through the use of information technology (IT).

The most difficult aspect of the process is producing the approximate budgets of time, etc., involved in the projects and of anticipated fee income. Moxley (1984) has produced a book which provides a detailed proforma approach, with associated software, to allow a systematic build-up of a tender and subsequent control of costs and time. An example of the approach is given in Figure 5.9.

Whether this particular framework is used or not, it is better simply to get started and allow the feedback loop to improve the reliability of the estimates made over time. It is in fact perfectly feasible to use computers to model budgets against the characteristics of various jobs, such as size, worktype, client charac-teristics (some are difficult), etc., although to the author's knowledge this has not yet been done.

In the collecting-data phase it is important, in the case of time sheets, that there is no pressure within the firm that might distort the veracity of the information given. For instance, if individuals are made to feel that they are spending too long on a project, the likely reaction is that they will load some of that time on to other projects where they think there is some leeway. This does nothing for the usefulness of the system, which will then suffer from the well-known problem in computing circles of 'garbage in garbage out' (GIGO).

Stage B Feasibility

The owner has decided to proceed with a new building or the rehabilitation of existing buildings and it is now necessary to establish the feasibility of such a project. The following is the full form.

B1 Administration

		Architect	QS	Structural Engineer	Services Engineer	Landscape Architect	Interior Designer	Legal	Owner	Owner advised by Architect	Hours/rate	Cost £	Totals (To be invoiced)
B1.1	Set up nucleus of design team, circulate reports and documents already approved by the owner.	X										X	To be invoiced
B1.2	Establish responsibilities.	X	X						X		NC	"	"
B1.3	Prepareplan of work and timetable.	X	X									X	"
B1.4	Define methods of coordinating information and recording it.	X	X									X	"
B1.5	Agree sources and the cost plan procedure.	X										X	"
B.2	**Surveys**												
B2.1	Commission detailed site survey or aerial photogrametric survey.	X										X	1500
B2.2	Obtain geological survey information by borings etc.			Z									400
B2.3	Research positions of public utilities, i.e. sewers, electrical, geo GPO culverts underground etc.				X								TBI
B2.4	Ascertain any easements from adjacent owners.							Z					
B2.5	Establish position of any old foundations or foul or poisoned ground, recently removed trees or other organic remains			X								X	TBI
2.6	Establish potential bearing pressures.			Z									600
B2.7	Consider ground drainage and water table characteristics.		X										200
B2.8	Consider mineral workings.		Z										NC

The owner and the architect (and other consultants) respectively shall provide the appropriate part(s) of the service indicated.

Owner (signed) *A. Bloggs*

Consultants (signed) *M. Steel*

Date *4 Feb '84*

Architect (signed) *M. Jenesk*

Project: *TECHOPERK*

Methods of payment:
Z Lump sum
Y Percentage of construction cost stage . . .
X Hourly rate
W Direct office cost plus percentage
V p per £100 of gross staff income
U Other (specify)

To summary 2700

Fig. 5.9 Example proforma for cost/time build-up

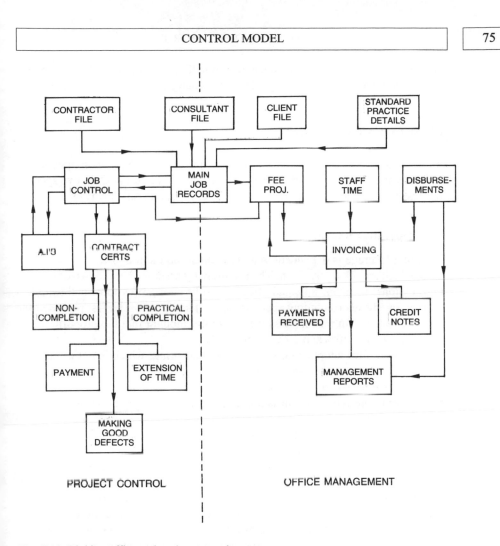

Fig. 5.10 Linking office and project control systems

In summary, the process can be very simple and the quality of data produced should improve as time goes on, but there is a necessity for effort to be extended in recording the data, etc., and it is this last aspect which must be justified. The value of the process is greatly enhanced if good quality data are obtained and analysed at various aggregate levels to support important decisions within the firm.

Before proceeding to the next section, it is emphasized that the firm's office management systems should not be viewed in isolation. There is a lot of common ground between the management of the firm's projects and the management of the office. Figure 5.10 (Lewis, 1991, p. 281) shows how 'main job records' can provide a focus and link for the two systems. Many of the details about clients and their projects can be entered just once and kept on these files and used for a variety of purposes. Other modules are linked and automatic updating occurs between modules if a variable, such a salaries paid to staff, changes.

5.3 ACCOUNTANT'S VIEW

Many firms will use accountants, and while it makes sense to use these specialists' expertise, some elements of their broad approach are of interest. Only two specific items will be treated here, namely operating leverage and ratio analysis.

5.3.1 Operating leverage

Operating leverage is dependent to a great extent on the proportion of the firm's costs, which are relatively fixed. The traditionally assumed breakdown of cost for a professional firm was an equal three-way split into: professional and technical salaries, overheads (including secretaries, etc.) and profit. The last provided the partners' income. In recent years it is generally thought that the proportions are more nearly 40%, 40% and 20%, respectively.

Unless the firm adopts a policy of hiring and firing, which is not usual, then professional and technical salaries are a relatively fixed item. Similarly, many of the firm's overheads are fairly fixed, such as support staff salaries and accommodation costs. The typical result is a high proportion of fixed costs, so that small changes in overall income, either positive or negative, have profound effects on the profit margin. Table 5.1 provides an example.

It can be seen that the very small increase in the income of only 1% produces a disproportionate increase in profits of 5%. It is quite feasible that the 1% increase in income could be produced by improved management techniques raising motivation among staff, hence the fact that no change in either salary costs or overheads is shown. The effect of operating leverage unfortunately works both for decreases as well as increases. Hence the annoyance of a partner with the young surveyor who agreed with a local authority to charge no disbursements in order to gain an instruction. It only involved a few hundred pounds, but in fact wiped out the majority of the profit element for that project!

There are other factors to take into consideration and the scenario in Table 5.2 shows a 5% increase volume in work supported by a similar increase in salaries,

Table 5.1 Effect of operating leverage

	Now	+1%	Then
Fees	100		101
Salary	80		80
Overheads			
Profit	20	+5%	21

Higher % fixed costs, the greater leverage on profits UP or DOWN

Table 5.2 Operating leverage and various factors

	Now	5% volume 5% up		5% fee rate	
Fees	100	→	105	→	110
Salaries	40		42		42
	60				68
Overheads	40				40
	20	+40%		→	28

Be aware of sensitivity of profit margin to **quite small** changes in volume/rate paid for work.

say, for overtime, and in addition shows a 5% increase in the percentage rate of charging – for example, the scale fee could have risen from 9.5% to 10% of the contract value. Both of these changes are quite small and one is fully supported by additional costs; however, the impact on profits is massive at +40%.

At a time when fee levels have been squeezed and, in many cases, overall fee income is declining it is critical to have an intuitive 'feel' for the effect on the profit margin if firms are not to get into difficulty. On a positive note it can be seen how quickly the benefits of good management practices would appear at the bottom line.

5.3.2 Ratio analyses

The use of ratios has already been mentioned at the start of this book when profit on fee income was suggested as a good performance measure because it can be tracked over time and is independent of the general volume of business being done. Various other measures are used within the accountancy profession to create norms which can then be used to check performance. Key areas which are often subjected to this treatment are unpaid bills and work done that is yet to be invoiced. These are critical areas for the cash flow of the firm, and without creating measures it is very difficult to keep control.

Taking outstanding bills as an example, the normal approach is to produce a ratio termed **debtor days**. This is calculated as follows:

Debtor days = (Outstanding monies/Total income) × 365.

It is difficult to determine the norm for an industry, but once established the firm can very quickly plot changes in its debtor days measure and in this way identify if matters are getting worse or better for the firm. If a problem is identified, then action can be taken. For instance, one firm that was having trouble with invoice payments changed its billing cycle to three weeks rather than a month and in this way cut across most other firms' financial cycles and actually triggered a rapid improvement in payments.

The key aspect of ratio analysis is carefully to select a measure based on easy-to-obtain data, but data which accurately reflects the position in a sensitive area of the firm's operations over which control is desired.

However well the firm runs its business, if time is not being well used at a personal level then the full potential of the staff will not be realized. The next section briefly considers this aspect.

5.4 PERSONAL TIME MANAGEMENT

In most firms it is normal for people to keep a diary and a list of 'things to do', and this is the minimum that most people can get by with and remain effective. After a time, so much pleasure is derived from crossing things off your list that there is a danger that you may write very simple things there, or things that are almost finished anyway, in order to be able to achieve a further psychological kick!

Over recent years there has been a trend towards the personal organizer, which allows flexible use of data in hard copy form so that, for instance, checklists can be interleaved between weeks of the diary and project sections can be created, etc. A step beyond this is to use a computerized diary which allows easy updating and can, if networked, take messages from other people. Whichever you use, it is important not only to make a note of deadlines, but also to put check dates in a month, two weeks, and a week before a major deadline falls due.

So far the picture painted has been rather reactive and, of course, it is possible, and desirable to plan your time ahead. One firm took the unusual step of asking each individual within the firm to plan his or her time out over the next month, and it used these data as a basis of its overall manpower planning for the firm as a whole. Areas where there was slack could be identified and people under pressure could similarly be pinpointed, given that the approach used made it possible to show a 110 or 120% input.

The other way in which time can be actively managed focuses on the work pattern of the day or week. With this approach an individual will identify the times of the day at which he or she is particularly alert, and programme in difficult problem-solving activities to these times. Other times of day will be earmarked for concentrated efforts to complete telephone calls, etc, and still other times set aside for meetings and other face-to-face interaction. In an extreme form this would appear to be fairly unrealistic, but clearly if the balance can be struck between a tempo of work that suits the individual and the demands of his or her projects, then general benefit can accrue. In this context it is worth mentioning the danger of encouraging a '9 to 5' mentality through the use of time sheets. It may be that an individual works better between $7 - 11$ am and $5 - 8$ pm. Provided that this is feasible, the firm should not be restrictive but should judge by output.

One of the main arguments underpinning suggestions of better time management are that it can greatly reduce stress by relieving the fragmentation of the day through positive actions, thus, creating a proactive approach rather than the feelings that there are just constant pressures from all directions. For instance, if you have planned your time out well in advance and someone telephones and asks you to arrange a meeting, you are then in a position to find a time that is mutually suitable.

The main point of relevance here is that, however good their systems are, if the individuals working within the firm are not efficient, it is simply not possible for the firm as a whole to achieve high levels of efficiency. When one considers the effect of a mere 1% increase in productivity, as described above, the potential latent in managing time better at an individual level can be seen.

5.5 SUMMARY

In this chapter we have considered various aspects of cost and time control within the firm, and have discussed the following key points:

- There is a wealth of information within the firm and from it the organization can gain a much better understanding of its business environment. In this way strategic management and marketing decisions can be based on more factual information than before.
- There is a cost in providing cost and time control and a subjective balance generally has to be struck.
- Creating budgets and judging performance using cost and time control systems can distort behaviour and great care is required when setting up systems if they are not to upset other aspects of the firm's operations.
- Wherever possible the firm's project and office management systems should be linked so that data are used efficiently.
- The profit margin is sensitive to relatively small changes in overall income, etc., and productivity must be achieved, ultimately, at a personal level.

Five years ago few firms had comprehensive cost and time control systems. Nowadays they are becoming increasingly common with real-time access for many people within the firm. This releases the potential for many positive actions, but some of the negative connotations are already beginning to appear.

For instance, one firm involved in the refurbishment of six housing units told staff part way through the job on site that they had spent nearly all the time allowed on that job and so would only visit monthly rather than weekly. Actions like this, where the cost and time control system is distorting professional judgement, are dangerous developments and any gains could be very quickly outweighed by the embarrassment and costs faced when inevitable mistakes end up in court.

With that one word of warning, it is fair to say that firms have the opportunity more than ever before to make informed decisions, and it would be nothing short of foolhardy not to grasp this opportunity wholeheartedly.

5.6 CHECKLIST

- Are budgets produced for each new job?
- Does the firm know its norms for key measures, such as 'debtor days'?

- Can and does the firm analyse its cost and time data to produce feedback for profit centres such as: client type, worktype and team performance?
- Are the cost and time systems distorting behaviour away from the firm's objectives?
- Has the firm done anything to increase the effectiveness of the personal time management of its staff?

PART THREE

Managing the firm's staff

Motivating professionals | 6

It has been stressed in Chapter 1 that, although efficiency is important and problems must be solved effectively, it would appear to be the motivational factors which account for more than half of the variation in the profitability of professional firms.

This is an issue of critical importance and one that is often given scant attention despite its wide-ranging effects. For instance, why do 'one man bands' account for around one quarter of all professional practices? Surely this is a strong indication of the failure of many professional firms to provide a motivating environment for their members to the extent that they not only perform at a lack-lustre level, but they actually leave the firm.

6.1 PROFESSIONALS ARE HUMAN

There has been a lot of research on what motivates people. This applies as much to professionals as to other occupational groups; they are humans, and have wants and aspirations.

6.1.1 Individuals' needs

The classic view, which has underpinned much of the research and theory in the area of motivation, is that of Abraham Maslow (1943). He tried to imagine the most fundamental categories of needs and produced the hierarchy given in Figure 6.1.

He also contributed some useful concepts in addition to the hierarchy itself.

- The hierarchy represents a rough order of priority, working from the bottom up. That is, if you are not safe, do not have enough to eat, then social relationships will probably not be critically important to you. For example, you might be quite willing to be rude in order to gain safety, or obtain sustenance.
- 'A satisfied need is no longer a motivator.' Once you have had enough to eat, hunger as a motivator recedes and perhaps thirst takes its place as the unsatiated need that motivates you to action.

Maslow's model is an oversimplification, but as a crude picture of the factors

Table 6.1 Self-assessment of motivational profile

Various ways in which your professional career might provide satisfaction to you are briefly described below. Please circle one number below each line to indicate how much you **want** the particular aspect in question, when you look to the future.

A second scale is provided in each case. Please mark this scale similarly to indicate how much of the aspect you actually **get** in your present employment.

(a) Friendship and mixing with others.

Great deal	Quite a lot	Some	Very little	Negligible
How much do you want?				
5	4	3	2	1
How much do you get?				
5	4	3	2	1

(b) Respect from others (at work and elsewhere) for your training/qualifications/job.

Negligible	Very little	Some	Quite a lot	Great deal
How much do you want?				
5	4	3	2	1
How much do you get?				
5	4	3	2	1

(c) Challenge to develop your ability to its fullest potential.

Great deal	Quite a lot	Some	Very little	Negligible
How much do you want?				
5	4	3	2	1
How much do you get?				
5	4	3	2	1

(d) A reasonable level of salary and other benefits.

Negligible	Very little	Some	Quite a lot	Great deal
How much do you want?				
5	4	3	2	1
How much do you get?				
5	4	3	2	1

(e) Association with people who have similar interests.

Great deal	Quite a lot	Some	Very little	Negligible
How much do you want?				
5	4	3	2	1
How much do you get?				
5	4	3	2	1

(f) Self-esteem through doing your work thoroughly and to a good standard.

Negligible	Very little	Some	Quite a lot	Great deal
How much do you want?				
5	4	3	2	1
How much do you get?				
5	4	3	2	1

(g) Opportunity to display creativity and individuality.

Great deal	Quite a lot	Some	Very little	Negligible
How much do you want?				
5	4	3	2	1
How much do you get?				
5	4	3	2	1

(h) Bonuses realistically related to high performance.

Negligible	Very little	Some	Quite a lot	Great deal
How much do you want?				
5	4	3	2	1
How much do you get?				
5	4	3	2	1

Table 6.1 Continued

	WANTS	GETS	NEEDS

1. Social aspect

Enter scores from (a)

Enter scores from (e)

Add two scores and

divide by two

Make scores %s by deducting

1 and multiplying by 25

Want % - Get % = Need %

Summary Social ☐% ☐% ☐%

2. Esteem aspect

Enter scores from (b)

Enter scores from (f)

Add two scores and

divide by two

Make scores %s by deducting

1 and multiplying by 25

Want % - Get % = Need %

Summary Esteem ☐% ☐% ☐%

	WANTS	GETS	NEEDS

3. Self-actualization

Enter scores from (c)

Enter scores from (g)

Add two scores and

divide by two

Make scores %s by deducting

1 and multiplying by 25

Want % - Get % = Need %

Summary Self-Act ☐% ☐% ☐%

4. Salary

Enter scores from (d)

Make scores %s by deducting

1 and multiplying by 25

Want % - Get % = Need %

Summary Salary ☐% ☐% ☐%

5. Bonus

Enter scores from (h)

Make scores %s by deducting

1 and multiplying by 25

Want % - Get % = Need %

Summary Bonus ☐ ☐ ☐%

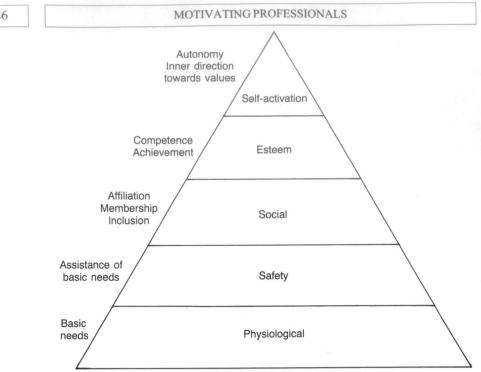

Fig. 6.1 Maslow's hierarchy of needs

involved it has proved robust to critical discussion for decades. The concepts are most easily understood in the realms of the physiological wants (hunger, thirst, etc.), but the 'higher' wants are possibly more important in the developed world.

This is simple to see if the second concept given above is re-examined:

- **'A satisfied need…':** most people in the developed world, almost certainly professional people, have satisfied their safety wants and their physiological wants in large measure.
- **'… is no longer a motivator':** as a result, the above categories of want are not likely to be central to a consideration of motivation for professionals.

Thus, for a professional the hierarchy could be expected to be represented by an inverted pyramid, as shown in Figure 6.2. This would not be universal in the

Maslow's   Temporary   Professional
                  secretary

Fig. 6.2 Alternative hierarchies

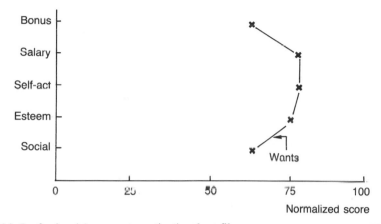

Fig. 6.3 Professionals' aggregate motivational profiles

developed world, for instance a temporary secretary might show a 'diamond' pattern.

To get a feel for the salience of the various factors, you should complete the questionnaire in Table 6.1.

6.1.2 Motivational profiles of professionals

A fairly recent study of 684 construction professionals (Barrett, 1989) measured their motivational wants. The results showed quite a stable aggregate profile, given in Figure 6.3, and provide a datum with which individuals can compare their own profiles.

The profile shows only the 'higher' motivational wants: social, esteem and self-actualization. Also included are 'salary' and 'bonus' representing money rewards, as steady income or performance-related pay respectively. These money factors will be discussed in the next chapter, but for the time being the focus will be on Maslow's higher wants.

What the professionals in the sample **wanted** was also measured, so too was the extent to which they **got** the factors, and lastly, the difference between the above two measures was calculated to give what have been termed **needs**. The needs are the degree to which the factors are unsatiated (given that, at the aggregate level, **wants** consistently exceeded **gets**, although this was not so for all individuals). **Wants** are particularly important, given that satiated wants do not motivate and so it is the unsatiated part that moves people. These additional measures are shown, together with **wants**, in Figure 6.4.

From this figure it can be seen that professionals' **wants** rise from social to esteem and finally to self-actualization, but when **gets** are deducted to give **needs** – that is, unsatiated wants – the rising trend is all the more evident.

It is fair to conclude that, in general, professionals will be motivated by

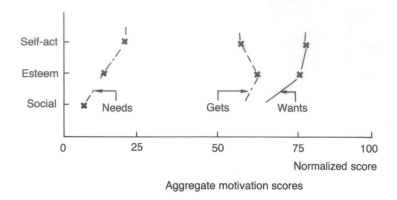

Aggregate motivation scores

Fig. 6.4 Professionals' wants, gets and needs

circumstances that allow the possibility of satisfying predominantly self-actualization wants and to an extent esteem wants, with social wants making little impact. In practical terms this means that professionals have a strong desire to reach their full potential, to be proud of what they have done and for their achievements to be recognized by other people.

There are some differences, but these do not change the above statement; rather they are matters of emphasis. The main difference discovered depended on the level of professionals in their organizations. This is shown in Figure 6.5.

It is clear that the **needs** of professionals are progressively **less** satiated as one goes down the hierarchy. This is due to the professionals **getting** more as they go up the hierarchy – what they **want** does not actually differ significantly across the different levels.

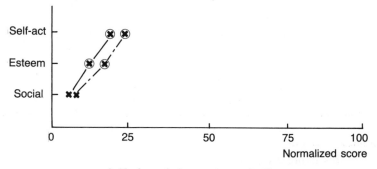

AoV of needs by employment category

Fig. 6.5 Variation in needs by level

So, it is the higher of Maslow's wants that are pertinent to professionals and these are increasingly satisfied as individuals progress up the hierarchies of their organizations. This bodes well for career progression as a long-term motivator. This is considered further in the next chapter.

6.1.3 Drag factors

The other, lower, wants can probably be discounted as motivators, but they remain relevant to the extent to which they can **impede** achieving success. This is a view put forward by Herzberg *et al.* (1959), who distinguished 'motivators' and 'hygiene factors', the latter being factors such as office support. Herzberg's work was based on a survey of 200 engineers and accountants, thus making it particularly relevant to the construction professions. He suggests that the **existence** of motivators brings forth effort and that the **absence** of hygiene factors depresses motivation (causes dissatisfaction). Further, motivators encourage people to grow in terms of their capabilities, so that, over a period, 110% effort can be achieved from 110% ability, whereas the provision of hygiene factors would at best result in, say, 70% effort (average?) from 100% ability.

It would be foolish, nevertheless, not to carefully attend to the hygiene factors that Herzberg lists (see Table 6.2).

6.2 GOAL-SEEKING BEHAVIOUR

6.2.1 Complex man

So far the models presented have given a fairly static view that is no doubt broadly correct, but the point has been made (Schein, 1972) that people are not very easy to categorize. Their wants change in their relative importance and overall salience; new motives are learned and different motives can be observed in the same person interacting in different situations.

At the root of this variability there are not only differences between the wants people have, but widely differing contexts and past experiences. Thus, although the wants of professionals are relatively stable, their behaviour will vary considerably because they are offered different opportunities or because their experience changes their perceptions of the same circumstances.

Table 6.2 Herzberg's motivators and hygiene factors

Motivators The job itself	Hygiene factors Environment
Achievement	Policies and administration
Recognition for accomplishment	Supervision
Challenging work	Working conditions
Increased responsibility	Interpersonal relations
Growth and development	Money, status, security

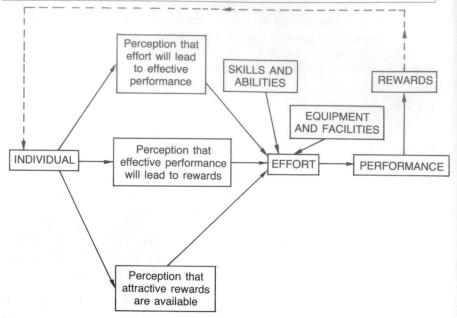

Fig. 6.6 An expectancy model

This **goal-seeking** view was first coherently propounded by Porter and Lawler (1968). A derivative of their model is shown in Figure 6.6.

The essence of the model is that individuals actively make choices as they endeavour to satisfy their wants, and in making these choices they take into account three factors:

1. **Instrumentality** – the degree to which effort expended on the given possibility will lead to good performance.
2. **Expectancy** – the probability that good performance in the area in question will lead to rewards.
3. **Valency** – the extent to which the rewards available are desired in terms of satisfying the individual's wants.

The judgements implied in the model will depend on contextual factors, such as the support the firm is likely to provide, and on past experience of the other people involved – for example, can they be trusted to do as they say they will.

This model summarizes the main factors to consider in any given situation. Similar assessments will be made simultaneously of various possibilities and an individual will draw from a variety of interactions to satisfy his or her wants. The implications of the model can be illustrated through the following simple example:

Henry, a recently qualified Building Surveyor, is told by his boss, Elizabeth, that he has a good chance of being promoted to Associate level within the firm within

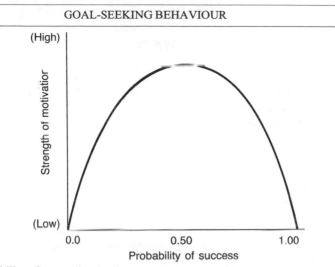

Fig. 6.7 Probability of success/motivation

the next six months, however she tells him that he will have to perform well on the five projects he is currently running.

How is Elizabeth's statement likely to affect Henry's motivation?

Henry has various options, but the components of the model allow a comprehensive review. He must ask himself: does he have the ability to do the projects well or are there overriding factors, such as poor contractors or inadequate support within the firm, which make this unlikely? If he does well, does Elizabeth have the power to grant the promotion and, if so, can she be trusted, judged from past experience? In any case, does Henry want the promotion?

Not only does this approach help the individual being managed to judge situations, it also can be of assistance to managers trying to motivate their staff.

In making probabilistic decisions a simple model is helpful in analysing the likely motivational effects of challenges placed before staff. This model is given in Figure 6.7.

If, for example, a person is assured of, say, a bonus, whatever the standard of performance, then no additional motivation will be called for. If, on the other hand, no matter how hard the person works, it will impossible to reach the level of output required to earn the bonus then, again, no additional effort will result. If the probability of success lies somewhere in between, then greater effort can be elicited, possibly with a maximum when the probability is 0.5.

6.2.2 Summary

So, we have moved on from a simple model of an individual's wants to a picture that includes many contextual factors within which the individual seeks to satisfy his or her wants by many and various means, involving simultaneous interaction with a large number of sources of stimuli.

6.3 THE EFFECTS OF EXPERIENCE

The influence of past experiences has already been mentioned. This is an important area for motivation because people do not make decisions afresh each time, but draw on their experience. The most profound influences on behaviour come from repeated success or repeated failure.

6.3.1 The effect of failure

If, for example, a person wants to be a design professional and enrols for a course of study to gain a professional qualification and fails the first-year exams, the reaction would probably be to try again. If failure occurs again and again, the individual will experience a phenomenon called **cognitive dissonance** (Festinger, 1957), – that is, a disparity between what the individual thinks should be happening and what is actually happening.

It has been found that people will not tolerate this 'dissonance' for very long. In order to overcome the problem something has to change: greater **effort** ('I think I'll try revising next time'); changed **expectations** ('perhaps I'll just have to take my time, maybe part-time study is the answer'); or the person's **goals** can change ('who wants to be an architect anyway?').

6.3.2 The effect of success

If, by changing one of the above variables, our student achieves success this will have a profound effect. A course of action that leads to success, and, when repeated, results in success again, leads to **positive reinforcement** (Skinner, 1953) – that is, the behaviour is confirmed and is very likely to be repeated.

The effect of a given experience also depends on the overall experience of the individual. It is analogous to dropping from a pipette a drop of red ink into a small glass of water and repeating the experiment but with a large container of water. The water in the small glass turns pink, but that in the large container absorbs the ink with no change in colour. So, too, with experience: if a person has a lot of experience it will take something quite spectacular to make an impact, but for a younger person with less experience each incident will make a mark.

6.4 THE MANAGER'S PERSPECTIVE

Obviously, to manage people effectively, one needs an understanding of what motivates them. Managers are interested more in actual **behaviour**, what people **do**, rather than why they are doing it. But, to predict behaviour it is better to have some understanding of the thought processes and likely orientations involved.

One issue is whether the manager's objective is to control or motivate. If a general management text on control is consulted it will show that control loops **checking compliance** with **defined standards**, etc. If a book written from a psychological perspective is opened at the chapter on control, the text will probably deal entirely with motivational issues. On the one hand there is controlling people to a standard, on the other, motivating them to high performance.

6.4.1 Managers' assumptions

Which approach is taken reflects underlying assumptions about the nature of the people being managed. McGregor (1957) categorized these assumptions into two groups, labelled Theory X and Theory Y, as shown in Table 6.3.

An important implication stressed by McGregor is that if you treat people based on the assumptions of Theory X then they will almost certainly end up fitting the description. Thus, taking the assumptions of Theory X can easily create a **self-fulfilling prophesy**. If you check closely on people because you cannot conceive that they will work unless pushed – certainly not to a good standard – then it is understandable that they will end up thinking 'Why should I bother? I'll do as little as I can get away with.'

But, yes, some people are lazy! The alternative, then, is to assume a Theory Y viewpoint until disproved. In this way the possibility of highly motivated Theory Y types being demoralized is avoided. In the specific case of professionals, judging from their motivational profiles as described in the last chapter, the likelihood is that they will be closer to the assumptions of Theory Y than to those of Theory X. A lot of damage could be done if a negative stance is taken.

6.4.2 Work as a part of an individual's life

Up to this point the analysis has been focused on people at work. Quite right, you

Table 6.3 Summaries of McGregor's Theory X and Theory Y

Theory X	Theory Y
1. Work is inherently distasteful to most people.	1. Work is as natural as play, if the conditions are favourable.
2. Most people are not ambitious, have little desire for responsibility, and prefer to be directed.	2. Self-control is often indispensable in achieving organizational goals.
3. Most people have little capacity for creativity in solving organizational problems.	3. The capacity for creativity in solving organizational problems is widely distributed in the population.
4. Motivation occurs only at the physiological and safety levels.	4. Motivation occurs at the social, esteem, and self-actualization levels, as well as physiological and security levels.
5. Most people must be closely controlled and often coerced to achieve organizational objectives.	5. People can be self-directed and creative at work if properly motivated.

might say, this book is supposed to be about management.However, when you are managing people they have an existence beyond work and the other parts of their lives can impact considerably on their performance at work.

Take the following example. John Cross was a surveyor with a high-powered firm. He worked from 7 am to 7 pm on a large volume of projects with great zeal for over three years. Even for the firm in question this was exceptional. One day he came into the office at the official opening time of 9.30 am and left sharp at 5.30 pm and continued to work these 'normal' hours thereafter. What had happened? He had got married and his wife had said 'no more'.

Schein (1988) uses the term **psychological contracts** to describe the way in which people balance their loyalties across various interactions. These are different from legal contracts, as they represent sets of mutual expectations that have developed over time. People would have such contracts with their managers at work, with the other members of their clubs, with their families, and so on. If managers are to fully understand their staff they need to view them as whole people who will only satisfy some of their wants at work. This limits the influence of the managers.

Work that throws light on this aspect was carried out in terms of **life interests**. Etzioni (1961) found that for manual workers only one-third of their life interests were associated with work! This rose to two-thirds for professionals. Thus, people managing professionals will have an attentive audience, but not to the extent of undivided attention. Professionals appear to seek to satisfy a great part of their wants through work, but they will critically assess the extent to which their current employment is facilitating their progress towards the achievements they desire.

6.5 SUMMARY

Professionals have high achievement wants and will seek to satisfy them through work. They will assess alternatives in the context of their experience and perception of the managers and the support available in the organization in which they are working. Professionals will react to multiple sources of stimuli and endeavour to balance their interactions to give themselves the optimum benefit in terms of satisfied wants.

So although they are working for the benefit of the firm, professionals will only do so effectively if, in parallel, they are also achieving their own ends.

The next chapter will examine the practical implications of the above in a professional firm and, in particular, the responses available that are likely to prove beneficial for the profitability of the firm.

Managing motivation | 7

7.1 INTRODUCTION

Moving on from a fuller understanding of the nature of professionals, albeit it in very broad, aggregate terms, we can now turn to the practical question: How do you motivate professionals?

First, we shall consider the motivation that can be derived from the actual work done, and discuss the motivational effect of the relationship between managers and their staff. The place of financial rewards in the equation will then be introduced, together with the possible use of inter-group competition.

The intrinsic motivation of the work will be considered in two parts: first, looking at day-to-day effects and, then, considering longer term career factors. The distinction here is between **goal** behaviour and **goal-seeking** behaviour (Hersey and Blanchard, 1982).

7.2 TASK DESIGN

What makes a job intrinsically motivating? This was a question Hackman and Oldham (1980) asked, and their answer, after much analysis, was that tasks should be assessed against the five dimensions given in Table 7.1. A high score for all the dimensions gives what they termed a high 'motivating potential score' (MPS). As shown in the table, the first three are combined and are given equal weight to each of the remaining two factors. The 'moderators' will be considered later.

Skill variety is very often available to professionals. For instance, a building surveyor could easily, in one day, write part of the specification, visit the site to supervise some building work, measure up some facet of the building and do some drawing back at the office together with some correspondence with clients. There are, of course, examples at the other extreme where a junior architect may spend days on end completing door and window schedules.

The above examples can also be related to **task identity**, which is the degree to which the person is involved in the whole job. Given that construction professionals

Table 7.1 Hackman and Oldham's dimensions

Core job dimensions	Critical psychological states	Outcomes
Skill variety		High internal work motivation
Task identity →	Experienced meaningfulness of the work	
Task significance →		High-quality work performance
		High satisfaction with work
Autonomy ————→	Experienced responsibility for work outcomes	
		Low absenteeism and turnover
Feedback ————→	Knowledge of the actual results of work activities	

MODERATORS
Ability and skill
Strength of employee's growth need
Context satisfaction

usually have a fairly well defined input into the overall construction process it is often possible, within the context of the firm, for an individual to handle a complete job. This is not necessarily the case and it may be that jobs will be broken down into specialist functions, a common example being the way quantity surveyors divide bill production into taking off, working up, etc.

Task significance will often correlate with the first two factors, but need not. For instance, it may be that a junior engineer in a small practice is given the task of making sure the tea and coffee supplies are kept well stocked. This can provide variety and identity, but is unlikely to be viewed as a significant task.

Autonomy and feedback are contextual factors and have to do with the attitude of the managers within the practice – although, in the case of feedback, this can be gleaned from a variety of sources. For instance, it is perhaps more motivating to receive praise from a satisfied client than it is to hear it second-hand through your boss.

So, if all of the above are satisfied then the task will have a high MPS. You can imagine, however, that, for instance, autonomy would be quite unwelcome if you were having difficulty with a task and did not want to be left alone! This raises a critical issue, which is that the above assessment produces a measure of a task's **potential** to motivate.

This potential will not be realized unless the individuals involved satisfy three conditions. They must **want** the opportunity to **achieve**, they must **possess** the **ability** to complete the task and, lastly, they must **not** be **constrained** by factors outside their control.

From the last chapter it will be evident that most professionals put great store in the higher level wants such as achievement or self-actualization, and so the first condition is likely to be satisfied. The issue of having the necessary ability will be looked at in more detail later in this chapter, which leaves the issue of 'drag factors' to consider in more depth now.

This could involve the absence of pieces of equipment such as computers, endoscopes, etc. It would appear, however, that the major factor in this respect is a provision of support staff. Of all the factors considered in the author's research (Barrett, 1989) this one emerged very strongly for reasons that are really self-evident. If professionals have technicians to work with them, they are less likely to have to engage in tasks patently lacking 'significance', such as photocopying and plan printing. Further, if there is good secretarial support the potential for the member of staff to achieve high levels of output is greatly enhanced. In addition, there is of course the undeniable pleasure of having people work **for** you.

It would be a mistake to stop the analysis there, because obviously the performance of the firm depends not only on the professional staff, but also on the support staff and it is important that their motivation is kept at high levels as well. It is quite clear, for instance, that some senior partner's secretaries are actively involved in partnership business and are able to act with quite considerable autonomy, on significant issues, in their employer's absence. In other firms the role is little more than that of the typist.

It is tempting to apply the model to support staff, but their motivational profiles have not been measured and the necessary conditions may not be met. In particular, they may not want greater responsibility. Remember, two-thirds of manual workers' **life interests** lay outside work, which gives an indication of how support staff may view work, but on balance there is probably massive potential to enhance the responsibilities, and also the contribution, of many of these members of the firm.

A further complication is that the salience of the various criteria vary over time, as discovered in research outside the construction industry and summarized in Figure 7.1 (Katz, 1978). From this it can be seen autonomy is definitely **not** wanted in the first few months of employment in a new job, and skill variety is of low importance. From about six months to around 20 years in employment all the factors slowly fall in importance. It was found, in contrast, that contextual factors, such as pay and compatibility with supervisors, remained of constant importance, thus these factors increased in relative importance over time.

It could be argued that Figure 7.1 does not apply to professional staff (except perhaps in relation to the start-up period) given the highly consistent results reported in the last chapter, where it could be seen that, irrespective of discipline or age, there was a high desire for achievement.

Now that the day-to-day effect of the work done has been considered, we shall turn to the effect of career progression as a motivation.

7.3 CAREER PATHS

Most professionals have either had first-hand experience of, or have watched other people, working tremendously hard in order to, first, qualify and, second, in the

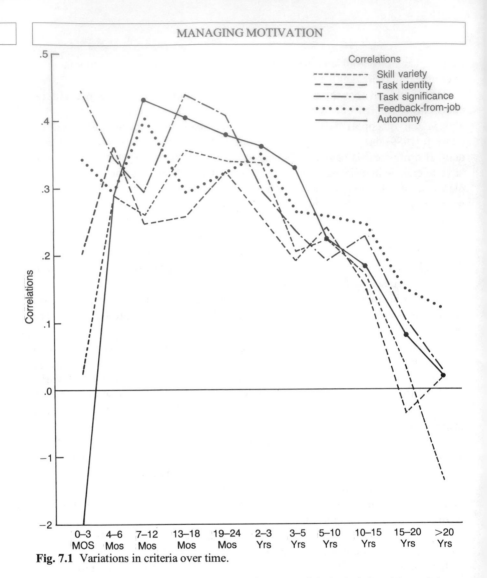

Fig. 7.1 Variations in criteria over time.

traditional partnership, progress to 'associate' possibly in their late 20s and then to continue into their early to mid-30s hoping to be admitted to the partnership. In many cases over a decade of sustained effort has been elicited in the hope of achieving partnership status. It is an incredibly strong drive and we shall see later in this chapter that the goal can indeed be highly intrinsically motivating once achieved, hence its desirability.

On the assumption that most individuals in a firm will be trying to progress upwards it is easy to imagine that problems can occur with organizations becoming top heavy or possibly awkward gaps appearing in the succession at senior levels.

David Maister (1982) has analyzed this numerically for the hypothetical firm

Table 7.2 Staff numbers of 'Firm X' over time

	Year										
	0	1	2	3	4	5	6	7	8	9	10 ...
Partners	4	5	6	7	8	10	12	14	16	20	24 ...
Associates	8	10	12	14	16	20	24	28	32	40	48 ...
Juniors	20	25	30	35	40	50	60	70	80	100	120 ...
Total	32	40	48	56	64	80	96	112	128	160	192 ...
New hires		10	10	10	10	20	20	20	20	40	40
Resignations		2	2	2	2	4	4	4	4	8	8
Annual percent growth in staff		25	20	17	14	25	20	17	14	25	20

100%   100%

shown in Table 7.2. The table assumes three levels of seniority within the firm: that is, juniors, associates and partners. It is further assumed that 80% of junior staff are promoted to associate level, on average, after four years. A further four years is taken for promotion to partner and in this case it is assumed that only 50% of the associates will be successful. The progression in both cases requires the learning of new skills and, particularly in the case of progression to partnership, the ability to handle client relations successfully, which precludes many people.

A further variable is the employment of new staff and this input is countered by resignations of those not promoted. There is an assumption that those not promoted will leave the firm and this is fairly realistic, but any given firm could rely on its own experience to make a judgement in this respect. The driving force for the analysis is the rate of new hires and growth occurs within the constraint of a fixed ratio between partners and associates of 1 : 2 and between associates and juniors of 1 : 2.5. (The actual proportions for any firm will depend on the type of work done and the degree to which the work can be proceduralized.)

The table then shows the firm growing steadily over a period of ten years, while keeping the relative proportions of staff types constant. It is possible to experiment with the table, changing assumptions and seeing what happens. For instance, if the firm was not growing, the potential to create posts at senior level would be limited and the loss of talented staff could be predicted. Although the picture appears complex the necessary assumptions can be quite readily made and with little effort various scenarios can be explored.

It is also possible to see from the table the effect of bringing people in at the higher levels thus precluding opportunities for existing staff and, something that would have to be included in a real exercise would be the retirement of partners which, unless managed very carefully, can be possibly the greatest source of disruption to the structure of a professional firm.

It may be that if the firm is growing very rapidly the supply of 'home grown' associates or partners may be insufficient, given the time necessary to acquire the skills to operate effectively at these levels. In this case it may well be necessary to recruit at these higher levels.

So, from the firm's point of view it is essential that the mix and numbers of staff are carefully assessed into the future, particularly as firms become larger. From each staff member's point of view the issues of critical importance are, both the **numbers** game described above and the **attitude** of partners towards promotions. To give extreme examples, one firm of quantity surveyors interviewed had seven professional staff, all of whom were partners. This is highly unusual but worked for that firm. Another firm had only one partner, and appeared to hold the potential for progression from the lower ranks, but, in that firm the sole partner had no intention of sharing power with anyone else.

If staff can see that there is a clear career route within a firm and that, if they perform well, they will be rewarded by promotion then this most potent source of motivation can be drawn upon. If, however, the firm does not plan its growth rate, recruits from outside at senior levels and does not honour the implied bargain with the staff, then they will either just serve time or quite possibly leave the firm. This eventuality may seem inconsequential, but when staff leave – particularly at associate level or higher – the firm loses more than just their physical presence. This is amplified in Table 7.3 (Barrett and Ostergren, 1991).

For small firms, plotting future growth is less easy due to the large effect one additional person has, but the principles still apply. When the firm is growing there is nothing but poor management to prevent career progression being made available to staff. Life in a shrinking market is much more difficult, but in a cyclical industry such as construction everything possible should be done to maintain goodwill and mutual respect even if the firm cannot, in the short term, create opportunities or even provide employment. There will come a time when the firm will want to be remembered for how it did its best for its staff in difficult circumstances.

The motivation available from the work done day-to-day and the possibility of

Table 7.3 Potential losses when staff leave

(a) The first loss is that of human beings, we can call it **'mass-escape'**. When some of the keypersons leave the firm to start something of their own, a lot of people feel that it's safer to go with them than to stay at the disintegrating firm. Another reason why a great number of people follow these keypersons is because they feel the pressure from the group.

(b) Besides 'mass-escape' the firm will lose markets when several people leave the firm, let's call it **'market-escape'**. Often a customer prefers to keep the consultant instead of hiring a special firm. Hence, if the consultant quits the firm loses its customer.

(c) A third kind of escape is **'technology-escape'**, i.e. the employee's knowledge will vanish, and also future progress in his area.

(d) We can also mention **'legitimacy-escape'**. The firm loses goodwill. It's not strange that rumours circulate when staff leave. This can lead to problems both when the firm recruits staff and when it sells its services.

(e) Last we can discuss **'culture-escape'**. When staff leave, it's possible that the atmosphere will change and result in a new culture.

career progression have both been considered. The effect of how managers deal with people will be looked at next.

7.4 MOTIVATION FROM MANAGERS

There are various ways of describing how managers deal with people. One very useful model has been developed in the area of leadership, which links well with the type of issue we have been discussing already. One of the key enabling conditions within Hackman and Oldham's model was that individuals should have the **ability** to do the task given to them.

The ability of those 'led' is a principal component of the leadership model developed by Hersey and Blanchard (1982). This model uses the ability level, for a particular task, of a member of staff to indicate the **appropriate** leadership style of the manager dealing with the person. It is a classic 'bricks and mortar' situation. There is no one right way to deal with individuals, rather the manager's approach must be tailored to suit the needs of those being supervised.

The question of alternative 'leadership' styles will be considered first, and then ability levels. Finally, the two aspects will be brought together.

The manager's approach can be viewed in terms of leadership style. Originally it was thought that leaders were either 'task' or 'people' oriented – that is, they were primarily concerned with either getting the job done or maintaining the morale, etc., of the people working for them. It was then found through some extensive research at the Ohio State University (Stogdill and Coons, 1957) that the two orientations were not in fact mutually exclusive but could occur in various combinations, and this gives rise to a grid of alternative styles with **task orientation** on one axis and **people orientation** on the other. This is shown in Figure 7.2, where the four main sectors created are labelled with key words, for example, a leader with a high task orientation and a low people orientation can be said to be 'telling' his followers what to do.

The essence of the approach is that there is no right or wrong style. All are equally capable of being appropriate, depending on some other factor. Before moving on to consider the other factor, namely follower maturity (ability), it is interesting to consider typical leadership styles using the grid of the framework for the analysis.

Many people have been tested for their style and 'average western man' tends to score highly in the 'cooperating' and 'supporting' sectors, that is, a predominantly people orientation. Technical people are generally found to exhibit a preference for 'telling' and 'cooperating', that is, a tendency towards task orientation.

Work with construction professionals has shown a consistent tendency towards a combination of the two above examples with 'cooperating' as the main style and 'telling' and 'supporting' as secondary styles. 'Delegating' very often does not figure at all, or at best receives a very low rating. These tendencies are summarized in Figure 7.3.

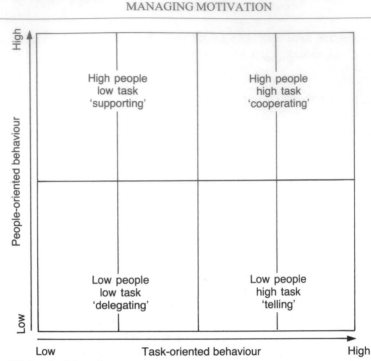

Fig. 7.2 Leadership styles

Hersey and Blanchard's major contribution was to suggest that, in assessing a manager's leadership style for appropriateness, it should be considered in the context of the ability levels or 'maturity' of the followers. They suggest that the followers' **maturity** is built up of two aspects, namely, competence and confidence. This is no different from the everyday expression about a person being 'willing and able' to do a job.

It is critical that the assessment is made in relation to particular tasks. Someone may be very good at designing purpose-made double-hung sash windows, but totally inadequate at calculating beam sizes for a cantilever projection. The question of ability levels has already been covered in some detail in Chapter 2, where a typical profile over time was provided, and is now repeated as Figure 7.4.

Taking scores of 3 to 4 on the y axis to represent a high level of ability for a particular task, it could be seen that a construction professional typically reaches this level within five years, having rapidly passed through a variety of ability levels

Average
western man

Technical
people

Construction
professionals

Fig. 7.3 Typical styles

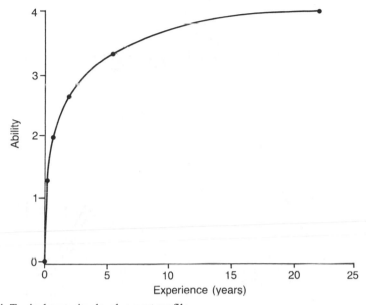

Fig. 7.4 Typical maturity development profile

in the early years. After five years there is only a slow improvement in competence.

Now that leadership styles and follower maturity have both been introduced, the next step is to consider how they relate. In Figure 7.5 a scale of M1 – M4 for follower maturity has been added beneath the leadership styles grid and a curvilinear line drawn over the grid showing the appropriate relationship between the leadership styles and the maturity levels. For instance, there is a point marked 'A' on the maturity scale and from this an ordinand has been struck vertically upwards until it meets the curvilinear line. This then indicates the leadership style that is appropriate for that level of follower maturity.

It can be seen that in broad terms that a low level of maturity requires a 'telling' style, high levels of maturity call for a 'delegating' style, and in between a 'cooperating' style is appropriate for moderately low levels of maturity, shifting to a 'supporting' style for moderately high levels of maturity.

A critical part of the model is that the leader should look for his or her followers' maturity levels in order to decide which style should be used. Referring back to Figure 7.3, it is evident that most construction professionals will be quite happy dealing with people with maturity levels from low to moderately high and will be particularly suited to dealing with people with moderately low maturity levels. They may well **not** be naturally suited to dealing with people with high maturity levels, given the dearth of emphasis allocated to the 'delegating' style.

Does this really matter? This question can be answered at two levels. The first factor is to consider whether this will result in a mismatch between the maturity

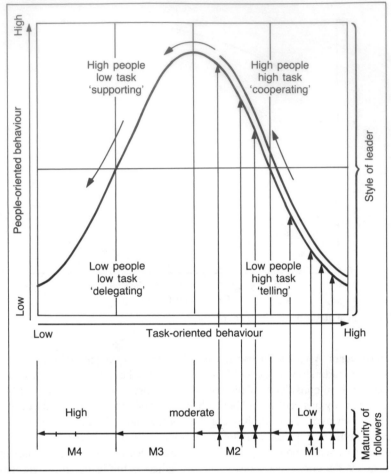

Fig. 7.5 Leadership style and follower maturity

levels found in the construction professions and the styles generally displayed. It can be seen from Figure 7.4 that professionals rapidly climb to high levels of maturity for given tasks and so, according to the theory at least, there is very likely to be a mismatch between the range of styles readily available to managers and the maturity levels of those with whom they are dealing.

Whether this really matters will depend on the implications of such a mismatch. There are two possible ways in which losses will be incurred. The first is that capable staff will inevitably be demotivated if they are not treated in a way that recognizes their ability and, secondly, managers are wasting their time and energy by not letting go when they should. Although fully delegating, and indeed 'telling', are high-risk styles, they are also the areas where extra output can be squeezed from those you are dealing with if used at the right time. So, if maximum motivation is to be achieved, the full range of styles should be used in response to the full range of maturity levels, but if this is to be done then managers must be adept at diagnosing the ability levels of those they are dealing with.

This argues for a dynamic relationship between leaders and their followers. It can be seen from the rapid development of followers that this is inevitable in any event. Managers can just follow their subordinates' changes in ability or can actively develop their followers by incrementally changing their style from 'telling' to 'cooperating' to 'supporting' and finally to 'delegating'; that is, the subordinate is moved from right to left over the hump of the curvilinear line. In this way, lasting staff development can be reliably achieved without the dangers attendant on 'throwing people in at the deep end', which is what happens if a shortcut is taken from a 'telling' to a full 'delegating' style. This can be very damaging to staff motivation, the firm's reputation and the firm's bank balance if things go wrong. If it happens to work out on one occasion you cannot be sure that this was not pure chance.

Leaders, therefore, need to diagnose their followers' ability levels to assess what their current leadership style should be. Taking into account the developmental view, it can then be seen that there is likely to be a demand for a manager to use a wide range of styles and show a high level of diagnostic ability if an appropriate input is to be made, especially when dealing with younger staff whose abilities are likely to vary rapidly.

In essence the leader is required to provide what the follower lacks, be it technical knowledge or confidence, so that the goals for which the leader is responsible are achieved (Schein, 1988, p. 134).

So, if managers are willing to make the effort to tailor their approach to their followers, it should be possible for them to make best use of their time: focusing their efforts where they are most needed and standing back where they can and, by doing this selectively for individuals a highly motivating work environment can be created for staff. But what about the managers themselves?

7.5 MOTIVATION OF MANAGERS

It is interesting to consider the position of managers themselves in terms of motivation. If we consider Hackman and Oldham's criteria for intrinsically motivating tasks it can be seen that managers will score highly on most of the criteria: their job is generally significant; they own their tasks and so can identify with them; there is a great variety of interaction with clients, staff, project involvement, etc.; their autonomy is greater than for most employees; and feedback is received from the many sources already mentioned.

It is likely that partners or directors of professional firms will have high growth needs and so, not only is their work likely to have a high motivated potential score, but they are also likely to find this stimulating.

Further, given the exposed position of managers of professional firms, where the firm's success is their success and the firm's failures are their failures, both in financial terms and in terms of self-esteem, it is not surprising that high motivation is usually evident among managers.

Another contributory factor to the managers' motivation is that, in the leadership equation, they would normally be in an ascendant position and it is known that, if at all possible, people do not like to be led (Rutte and Wilke, 1985). By being the leaders, the managers in professional firms escape subjugation, but in addition gain self-esteem from their authority over other staff.

Given that senior members of a firm are highly likely to have come through a technical route, there is a possibility that they may not feel comfortable with managerial roles and may in fact find it difficult to deal with staff. This could undermine some of the satisfaction outlined above.

Overall, for the managers within a professional firm it seems fair to suggest that they are likely to be highly motivated.

This leads to the thought, 'Why not make everyone a manager?', which, of course, seems naive but in fact can, in some respects, be achieved through company share schemes and there are, in fact, some practices where the great majority of staff are partners. Militating against this, of course, is the desire of existing partners not to share the profit distribution with more people. In so doing it is probable that the profit to be shared is not as a great as it could be.

7.6 MONEY AS A MOTIVATOR

It is common experience that money does motivate people, but it is important to dig slightly deeper. People don't (generally) eat money or burn it for warmth. It is in reality what money can buy or what it represents that is important. Relating this point to Maslow's hierarchy of wants it is apparent that money can satisfy physiological needs such as hunger and thirst, it can provide safety and shelter in terms of accommodation by paying the mortgage, it can possibly assist some social aspects by allowing membership of clubs, etc., but here the potency of money is reducing. Money can raise the esteem with which the individual is held in some people's eyes, although it can be counter-productive in relation to others. Money may satisfy self-esteem needs although actual achievements are likely to be more important here, and in terms of self-actualization money itself would probably be at best a fairly unimportant by-product.

Certainly, in the case of staff, it is likely that **equity** will be a major consideration rather than the absolute level of an individual's salary *per se*. That is, if a person's pay is even marginally below that of someone else, who is perceived to be doing the same job, then the first person is likely to be dissatisfied. In this way pay can operate as a hygiene factor undermining motivation if it is not perceived as equitable, but not particularly producing motivation if it is thought to be fair.

An area in which money can possibly be used as a 'motivator' is through performance-related pay. This is confirmed by Figure 7.6, which is repeated from

Figure 6.4 and shows Maslow's factors, as well as money factors, measured for construction professionals (Barrett, 1989). It can be seen that 'bonus' (performance-related pay) is the area where the greatest unsatiated **need** is found. Importantly, this is due to a particularly low **get** rating, not an especially high **want** rating. Thus, bonuses must be used carefully and selectively, but there is also a lot of potential in this area to release further motivation. This is especially so in the public sector, as shown in Figure 7.7. In Figure 7.8 the analysis is by level in the firm and it is noticeable that **bonus** is the only factor that is less satiated for staff in the middle of the firm than for those lower down. It would appear that there is a particularly strong requirement for bonuses on the part of, say, associates, which is not often fully satisfied.

If performance-related pay is to work effectively it is necessary for various conditions to be satisfied. These can be drawn from the expectancy approach to motivation shown in Figure 6.6 of the last chapter. Is the bonus worth having, or, for instance, does the level of taxation undermine its worth? Can the bosses be trusted to play fair and not make the higher level of performance achieved the new base line? Will further effort result in a level of performance that will earn a bonus, or is there inadequate back-up, or would someone else get the credit?

The use of bonuses can cause various problems if they are not handled well. Traditionally firms would give *ex gratia* bonuses, if they could be afforded in any particular year, to those members of staff that the partners felt had done well, but the system was shrouded in mystery and depended on mutual trust. In this context, Burstein and Stasiowski (1982) suggest that bonuses should be worth at least a month's salary and that not more than 20% of staff in any one year should be included. Thus, presumably, the bonuses remain significant and carry some measure of esteem.

More recently some firms have introduced formal systems where targets are

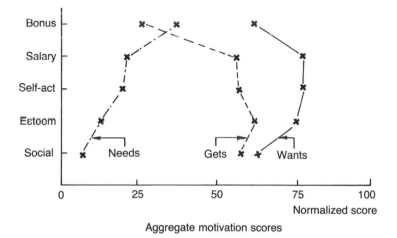

Fig. 7.6 Professionals' wants, gets and needs

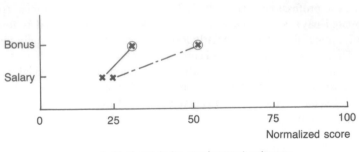

AoV of needs by employment category

Fig. 7.7 Money needs by employment category

set and known profit shares will emerge if certain levels of performance are achieved. This clearly could work, but various problems are known to have arisen which have been touched upon already in Chapter 5, and are considered in more detail below.

One possible problem is that merely informing staff more openly of the firm's financial matters can in itself lead to dissatisfaction. For instance, there was a case of three associates in a large firm who, on the introduction of a bonus scheme, came to the conclusion that they were jointly generating about half of the income of the

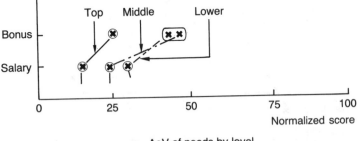

AoV of needs by level

Fig. 7.8 Money needs by level

firm, but despite this they could still not reach the threshold that would trigger a bonus payment. As a result they became dissatisfied and left to set up their own practice.

Additionally, operating bonus schemes at an individual level, although perfectly possible given the sophisticated cost and time management systems that many firms now have, can create conflict within groups of people who – in the firm's interest – must work closely and harmoniously together. If each member of the team is striving to make his or her contribution stand out, this can obviously be very destructive. Several firms have now been through the learning experience of first operating individual bonuses, confronting this particular problem and moving on to bonuses assessed at the group level. Used in this way bonuses can provide a very real stimulus for a group to work together effectively.

An example of how this sort of problem can arise between organizational building blocks, such as departments, was noted at a firm that had created specialist departments with specific skills and had centred the bonus system specifically on work done within each department. Unfortunately the two initiatives did not always work together. When, for instance, a very lucrative commercial project came to the partner who would normally deal with local authority housing, the operation of the bonus scheme made this partner very loathe to hand the project to the 'correct' department, and instead there was a tendency for only projects likely to have low profit margins to be redistributed to the departments to which they logically belonged.

The above links to a final general problem with performance-related pay, which is that there will be a distortion of behaviour within the firm towards factors that can be easily measured, termed **over-measurement** (Etzioni, 1964), unless positive action is taken to give credit for aspects that are not so easy to quantify. If the only fact that is taken into consideration is the income being produced by project work, then staff will tend to put very little time or effort into longer term matters such as researching speculative areas of work for the future, putting effort into improving the systems of the firm, making efforts to maintain good staff morale, etc. The tendency will be for the culture of the firm to become short-term oriented, reactive and opportunistic.

If the firm wants individuals to take actions within a longer time frame on a broader range of issues, then it must acknowledge and reward actions in these directions.

Drawing from White (1981), John Child (1984) has suggested the summary, given in Table 7.4, of the main dimensions around which choices on payment/bonus systems can be made.

7.7 GROUP COMPETITION

The discussion so far has been predominantly at the level of the individual, but it is well known that the forces within groups can have a strong effect on how people

Table 7.4 Choices in the design of payment systems*

1 Simplicity	*or*	**complexity**
Example: flat time rates or traditional piecework without additional features.		*Example:* job evaluation in conjunction with various types of incentives, bonus or profit-sharing schemes.
In a period of change and pressure, makes it easier for managers to exercise control and keep track of costs.		Provides management with more options to respond to various requirements; but difficult to get the balance right or predict cost implications.
2 Standardization	*or*	**differentation**
Example: all employees on flat time rates and grouped into few job categories.		*Example*: extensive use of merit-rating; or executives allowed to choose between percentage of their pay made up by profit-related bonus.
Ease and low cost of administration. Avoids risk of charges of favouritism.		Recognizes individual differences and adapts payment system to these, thus enhancing motivational potential.
3 Relatively fixed or rigid	*or*	**flexible and adaptable**
Example: measured daywork.		*Example*: corporate profit-sharing or added-value bonus system.
Attractive in terms of maintaining discipline and control in face of change and pressures.		Attractive in terms of avoiding confrontation with workforce.
4 Attempt to influence motivation or increase individual performance	*or*	**emphasis on building harmonious collective relationships**
Example: output incentive schemes.		*Example*: plant-wide bonuses, profit-sharing.
Maximises motivational potential and helps to control direct costs in face of intensifying competition.		Conducive to cooperative, harmonious industrial relations, and to achieving flexible manning.

*Based largely on the discussion in Michael White, *Payment Systems in Britain*, Gower Press 1981, pp. 37–8.

behave. This section looks specifically at group competition as a potential means of eliciting higher effort from staff.

It is a well-known phenomenon that if groups are created then a group's perception of itself becomes more and more positive, but the group's perception of other groups deteriorates and these changes can result in inter-group competition, or, if it is not handled properly, conflict. The following extract summarizes an experiment (Sherif and Sherif, 1956) with children, which demonstrates the way in which groups can form and conflict can arise with other groups. A clear message is that those in charge may be able to initiate the formation of groups, but they may not be able to control the behaviour which ensues!

'Bull dogs and red devils'

In 1949 Sherif and Sherif designed an experiment to demonstrate group formation, in conditions that were as far as possible controlled. Their work is an excellent example of experimental method outside the laboratory. They selected a sample of twenty-four boys for an eighteen-day summer camp in Connecticut, U.S.A. So that grouping among the boys should be determined only by experimental factors, and not by differences in factors outside the experiment like previous friendships or different ages, such possible influences had to be ruled out. This was done by selecting boys the same or nearly the same in:

Age (about twelve);
Social origin (lower-middle-class American families);
Educational experience and opportunity;
Religion (Protestant families);
Intelligence (middling test results);
Normal boyhood (no 'behaviour problems');
Being unknown to one another beforehand.

Intrinsic personality differences and shared interests which might create personal likes or dislikes had still to be eliminated. So for the first three days at the camp the boys were left to sort themselves out spontaneously into small groups of new pals. Then they were officially divided into two groups for the purpose of the experimental stage, the division deliberately splitting up these incipient friendships so that within the two arranged groups spontaneous attractions would be minimized.

The camp organizers closely watched the boys' behaviour, and made notes of significant happenings when they were out of sight, but the boys were not aware that the control exercised was for any purpose beyond that of the usual summer camp. Sherif himself took the role of a caretaker. Records compiled included charts of who chose to sleep in adjacent bunks, to sit together at meals, to take part in games, etc. The conditions having been set, the experimental stages could begin, namely - *Stage 2: experimentally determined forming of groups,* and *Stage 3: experimentally determined forming of the relationship between groups.*

Stage 2: The forming of groups (five days). After the division into two lots of twelve boys, each half was assigned an identifying colour, red and blue, and each chose a separate bunkhouse for itself. Straight away they were sent off on hikes in opposite directions, to counteract any resentment at new buddies being parted and to begin the experimental conditions. All activities were henceforth organized separately. Eating was at separate tables, camp chores done on alternate days, separate camping trips and swimming arranged.

The effect was striking. Two collections of twelve boys turned into two close-knit groups. They chose group names, the Bull Dogs and the Red Devils. Each group found its own 'secret' hide-out in the woods, and its swimming place. Each preferred certain songs, each preferred particular ways of doing things, like making lanyards. Each tended to refer to its bunkhouse as 'home'. Certain boys took the lead in each group, and enforced types of punishment peculiar to each: for example, offenders among the Bull Dogs were made to remove stones from the group's swimming pool, a sanction utilized by their leader and accepted as fair by the group. Moreover, the incipient friendship choices of the first three days were often completely reversed. The boys were given questionnaires asking which other boys out of the whole twenty-four they now liked best, so that the sociometric pattern of choice could be compared with what it was before.

Table   *Friendship choices*

	Choices made by	Choices (%) received by	
		eventual in-group	eventual out-group
End of stage 1	Eventual Red Devils	35.1	64.9
(first three days)	Eventual Bull Dogs	35.0	65.0
		in-group	out-group
End of stage 2	Red Devils	95.0	5.0
(five days)	Bull Dogs	87.7	12.3

These results show the overwhelming concentration of choice within the boundaries of each group, former likings for boys now in the other groups having been largely forgotten. Indeed, comments were beginning to be heard in each group about 'their lousy cabin', or 'our pond is better'.

Stage 3: The forming of relationships between groups (five days). To test whether inter-group friction could be created, a series of competitive games and contests between the Bull Dogs and the Red Devils was now announced: in fact, some boys had been asking for this. Each day began with a tug-of-war, there were ball games, and so on. The overall winners were to receive twelve four-bladed knives as prizes. At first there was 'good sportsmanship' and cheers for the other team, but soon '2-4-6-8-, who do we appreciate' became '2-4-6-8-, who do we appreci-hate'. Name-calling began, the losing Red Devils labelling the winning Bull Dogs as 'dirty players', 'cheats', and worse. The Bull Dogs showed increased pride in their group; but the Red Devils became frustrated and a little disorganized. But later attacks by the Bull Dogs produced a freshly cohesive rallying of the Red Devils.

Finally, when the Bull Dogs won the inter-group prize, the experimenters proposed a party in the evening to let 'bygones be bygones'. Refreshments were set out in the mess hall, half of them delectable and the other half crushed and unappetizing. By careful timing the Red Devils were allowed to arrive first. They took the good half and tucked in. The Bull Dogs arrived. Shocked by the situation as it appeared to them, they refrained from hurling their crushed cake at the Red Devils only when they realized it tasted good anyway. But the meal broke up in a series of fights. Next morning after breakfast the Red Devils deliberately dirtied their table, it being the Bull Dogs' turn to clear up; so the latter retaliated by making a bigger mess and leaving it. At lunch the two groups were soon lined up throwing food and crockery at each other.

Here the experiment finished as such. But it took two days' exhortation and discipline from the staff to stop open fighting: and efforts to unite the camp by mixing the groups in games and activities and in a softball game against an outside team were only partially successful by the time the camp ended.

[Adapted from Sherif and Sherif, *An Outline of Social Psychology*, 1956; and Rohrer and Sherif (eds.), *Social Psychology at the Crossroads*, 1951, by Handy, 1985, pp. 148–50.]

It is surprisingly easy to create groupings within an organization: a flight of stairs will suffice, with those people on one floor identifying themselves as separate from people on other floors; membership of different professional disciplines is equally effective.

Competition between groups can, of course, be beneficial if it raises the general level of performance. Handy (1985) states that such competition can set standards, stimulate within-group effort and 'sort out' or allow comparative assessment. This last feature is most likely to lead to conflict. A key factor here is whether the possible rewards are fixed or whether **open competition** is possible.

If the groups are competing for a fixed 'cake' then the likelihood of conflict arising is high and, if it does, the groups will tend to interfere with the efficient running of other groups when they can. Disinformation will arise and many negative implications are likely.

If, however, open competition is possible – for instance, the groups may work in different markets either in terms of clients, or geographically – then in these circumstances the competition can be productive.

7.8 SUMMARY

This chapter has looked at the practical techniques available to motivate staff through well-designed tasks, carefully managed career paths, effective leadership and the careful use of financial rewards. Lastly, the positive possibilities of inter-group competition have been introduced.

7.9 CHECKLIST

- Are the tasks of the firm designed to be motivating as well as expedient? Are they being done by the right people?
- Do the managers in the firm really vary their leadership styles depending on the level of expertise of the staff being dealt with?
- Are there realistic career paths within the firm? Do staff know about them? Will they cause log-jams in the longer term?
- Is the potential of bonuses being harnessed (with care)?
- Does the firm encourage open competition?

Managing change 8

8.1 WHAT IS CHANGE?

Professional firms in general, and those involved in construction in particular, have faced unprecedented change over the last decade and the rate of change appears to be accelerating towards the end of the millennium.

Major structural changes can be seen occurring in three main areas: the markets for professional services; the nature of client demand; and, lastly, developments in information technology.

8.1.1 Change in markets

A whole range of factors within the environment of the professional firm have changed over the last 20 years in such a way that the combined effect has been to push professional firms away from their traditional modes of operating towards a more business-like approach. This is summarized in the force field analysis shown as Figure 0.1 in the Introduction.

In addition, there is the breaking down of trade barriers between the domestic UK economy and the remainder of western Europe from the beginning of 1993. As the Lay Report (RICS, 1991) points out, this will result in our local economy becoming a twelfth part of a much larger economic system. This particularly noticeable change is in fact part of a trend towards globalization, and business with the EFTA countries is already building and so too are relationships with eastern European countries as they move towards market economies.

8.1.2 Change in client demand

It is well known that many of the features of the 'traditional' approach to construction used in the British construction industry can be traced back 100 years, and in some instances still further to the time of the Guilds. For all that, there have been significant changes over the last 20 years and many alternative procurement systems are now available. This process of services being created, developed and then declining has been identified in the service management literature in terms of

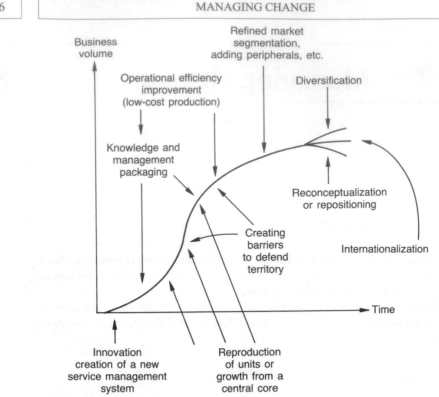

Fig. 8.1 Service life cycle (Sibson, 1971)

service cycles (e.g. Webb, 1982; Foster, 1986). See Figure 8.1.

This view stresses that the longevity of existing services cannot be taken for granted and professional firms, if they are to survive in the longer term, need a marketing orientation which makes them sensitive to changing client demands. One major identifiable trend is the increasing demand for professional advice, which takes a particularly broad view. This is discussed in more detail in Chapter 9.

8.1.3 Changes in information technology

There have been rapid advances in the availability of information technology which pose both threats and opportunities to the construction professions. On the one hand, there is the danger that the professions will become deskilled as information technology makes expertise more widely available, possibly through expert systems.

On the other hand, the same technology holds out the possibility for firms to greatly enhance the quality of the services they have to offer. In addition, information technology can give firms great flexibility in terms of work patterns along the dimensions of time, place and content. Gone are the days when dictation to a short-hand typist took place in one's office and any corrections that had to be made demanded retyping. Now professionals can dictate work, make phone calls or link up with computers almost anywhere, leave work to be done by others at different times and very quickly manipulate existing documents by moving text, etc, around. Thus, work can be made to fit in with the workers and quick, accurate responses to a client's request can be provided.

8.1.4 Summary

From the above it should be clear that the claim that the construction professionals are facing unprecedented change was not made lightly. In all of the above instances the changes are already upon us and are affecting more and more firms within the industry.

The one factor that has not been mentioned so far in this chapter is that of 'people', that is, the individuals involved in the construction professions. The remainder of this chapter will consider the effect of major changes on the people involved.

People cannot be seen as a side-issue if Lewin's (1947) suggestion is taken seriously, that if you dig deeply enough into any problem you will come eventually to people! There is no point in firms making grand plans for change if they do not give equally serious consideration to how to manage the change process within their organization. No change process is easy. It may appear blatantly obvious to the proponents, but it is likely to appear just as unreasonable to many of those affected. As a result the process is rarely comfortable.

The remainder of this chapter will look at the reasons for resistance to change, techniques for overcoming that resistance and a model for producing lasting change. Finally, the value of change compared with stability will be considered.

8.2 RESISTANCE TO CHANGE

8.2.1 Levels of change

As mentioned earlier in this book, from a managerial perspective – although attitudes are interesting – it is behaviour, or people's **actions**, that matter in the end. Much of the resistance to change goes unnoticed because it is assumed that once people are persuaded of the correctness of a point of view they will then, in fact, change their behaviour. The process is more complex than this and Figure 8.2 shows the various stages from the changing of the person's knowledge base, which in time will have an impact on his or her attitudes and eventually result in changed behaviour patterns, provided peer pressure can be overcome.

The effects of the model can be seen in the profession's response to computers. Initially people would readily admit that computers could lead to greater efficiency but still tended to have a negative attitude towards them. Slowly this attitude has changed as home computers have become quite normal, and it is now commonplace to find individuals within practices who are very willing to use computers to support

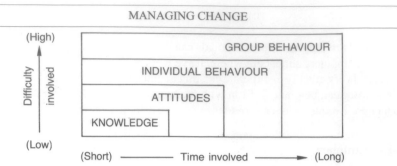

Fig. 8.2 Changing behaviour as well as knowledge (Kast and Rosenzweig, 1981).

their work, but it may be that in a (rapidly decreasing) number of practices the norms within the practice are still inclined towards hand drafting and so the willingness of the individual is contained.

8.2.2 Social resistance

The above model argues for a sustained approach to managing change which goes beyond merely winning the argument. A key stage in the process is to overcome group pressure, which should not be underestimated. In the past many firms in different disciplines have sent individuals on courses to change their attitudes and skills. When they have returned to the parent organization it is common experience that they had little impact on the organization as a whole (Argyris, 1962).

A measure of the potency of group pressure was provided by experiments carried out by Solomon Asch (1955) in which he created a situation where an individual being tested was put in a group of other people who had been told beforehand to give the incorrect answer to a very simple question which involved comparing lengths of lines on cards. The answers were patently obvious, and, on their own, the 'guinea pigs' made no mistakes. When one other person was involved in giving an incorrect answer, it made no difference; but when in a group of three, 14% of the 'guinea pigs' gave the wrong answer to be in line with the other group members. In groups of four this increased to 32%. Those who did not fit in with the 'group norm' – that is, the incorrect response – exhibited extreme signs of discomfort with sweating, stammering, etc. It should be mentioned, however, that there is subsequent evidence that professionals, such as engineers, who are trained to come to independent judgements on difficult issues, are not as susceptible to such pressure (Perrin and Spencer, 1981).

For all that, the pressure is there. For example, the manager who joined a department and endeavoured to get his staff to work through their lunch hour, as he did, very soon found himself taking a break too!

8.2.3 Conservatism

Another source of resistance to change has been termed **dynamic conservatism**, which reflects the energy and innovation some people will put into maintaining the status quo. This is confirmed by Lansley (1985), who found that research is only well received by the construction industry if its suggestions are: familiar, focused, self-contained and backed by people or bodies of high standing. Not a recipe for rampant innovation!

To a great extent this conservatism will be founded on sunk costs, which is the investment people have made in the past to produce the status quo. For instance, continuing our example of the use of computers, if individuals have developed hand-drafting skills to a high degree then it is only natural that they should resist moves that will make this skill irrelevant. Similar arguments can apply to changes in structure where senior personnel with great power will be unlikely to support changes that will reduce their significance in the organization of the future.

In addition to the above potential losses against past investments, there is the question of costs attached to introducing further changes within an organization. Many of the adverse reactions to change will be rooted in a fear of the unknown, and Figure 8.3 gives a view on related changes in learning, confidence, confusion and anxiety springing from the introduction of change. It can be seen that confusion and anxiety are likely to be high initially and decline as the learning curve rises. The diagram suggests that confidence will also be high initially, on the assumption that those involved thought the change was a good idea, but as time goes on the full implications will be realized and the discomfort felt will undermine confidence although it is anticipated that it will begin to rise again after a time.

8.2.4 Summary

The consistent message is that the change process must receive a sustained effort, over time, if it is to be successfully achieved. There is no point in saying, 'But you

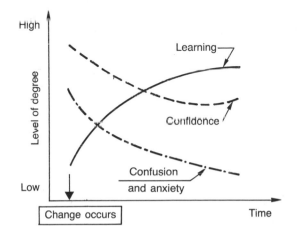

Fig. 8.3 Impact of change on confidence, confusion and anxiety (based on Newman, 1975)

agreed to it, why are you backing out now?' It is better to be ready for this sort of development and to react positively to it.

It is important to appreciate the very real and potent resistance there will often be to any proposed change. There is no point in just being right. It is necessary to overcome the resistance through a sustained effort if the initiative is to be successful. The next section considers alternative approaches to overcoming any resistance to change.

8.3 OVERCOMING RESISTANCE TO CHANGE

Various facets will be considered: communication, involvement and power.

8.3.1 Communication

Clear communications are essential if the **process** of change is not to be blocked by misunderstandings. Those managing change need to reinforce their message, code it carefully for the recipients and actively seek feedback (Adair, 1973) as already described in Chapter 4 in relation to marketing.

Canter (1983) stresses the importance of **how** a change is presented. She advises 'change agents' to define initiatives, as set out in Table 8.1.

8.3.2 Involvement

The question of involvement is important (Vroom, 1974). There are two main facets to this issue: knowledge and commitment. For slight problems or straightforward changes the manager can simply make a personal decision, but although this would meet the knowledge criterion, it would not create commitment. This may not matter if, for example, a firm decides to share an accountant with another firm in the same building, but if the everyday work of the firm is implicated, say, by moving office location, then it would be well to involve staff, if only to

Table 8.1 Canter's advice to change agents

PRESENTING CHANGE SUCCESSFULLY
triable
reversible
divisible
concrete
familiar
congruent
sexy

increase the chances of gaining their commitment.

For complex, difficult changes, such as those typically produced by strategic planning exercises, it is wise to involve more people in order to create a greater pool of knowledge. It would be dangerous for an individual, or small group, to produce a solution alone. In addition to knowledge there is the extra benefit to be gained from bringing a range of problem-solving approaches to an issue (Belbin, 1983; Powell, 1991).

Research into alternative communication networks – already mentioned in Chapter 3 and shown in Figure 3.5 – supports the above considerations.

Obviously there is a cost attached to involving more people, but the potential benefits are rigour and commitment.

8.3.3 Power

However good a proposed change, and however well presented, there is still likely to be a need to persuade some people. This introduces power as an important factor. Handy (1985) has suggested a continuum that could be said to range from 'nice' to 'nasty'. He suggests that power can be based on personality (charisma), expertise, position, resource control and, lastly, physical threats. In managing a change process it is clearly better to use 'nice' power sources first and 'nasty' bases only when unavoidable (if at all!) if long-term, self-maintaining change is desired. The less explicit the persuasion the more effective it can be. For instance, if greater teamwork is desired, arranging the spaces in the office to facilitate this is much more likely to succeed than telling or asking people to work in teams. Handy terms this **managing the ecology** of the organization.

8.3.4 Summary

The above considerations are all important factors in achieving change. It is also desirable for changes to be self-maintaining if at all possible. The next section will look at this aspect in more detail.

8.4 ACHIEVING LASTING CHANGE

8.4.1 Model

The classic model in this area is the three-stage model proposed by Lewin (1947):

- unfreeze
- change
- refreeze.

This model explicitly acknowledges the importance of making efforts before and after the change to achieve lasting results.

(a) *Unfreezing*

The unfreezing stage is intended to prepare people for the change by breaking down their fixed views of the existing situation. Management consultants generally insist on a client survey which can provide a potent basis for change by undermining any complacency in the firm being studied. Similarly, a post-occupancy evaluation of a building design could be an effective way of persuading a design team that it should reconsider its approach.

The actions to unfreeze can be pleasant, such as removing to a country club to allow free thinking away from the office. They can also be very unpleasant, such as sacking key people in the existing organization, or bringing into disrepute the opinions of key opponents of the proposed change (Johnson, 1990).

(b) *Changing*

In the actual change phase, symbolic actions and positive reinforcement are important. Johnson (1990) stresses various ways in which symbolic actions can make a massive difference. In one local authority the chief executive sat at the reception desk for an hour every Monday morning and dealt with the public to show the importance he attached to a customer care initiative. Stories like these circulate within the organization and are very persuasive. At the other extreme, if there is any hint that top management is not fully behind a proposal it is almost certain to fail. The difficulty faced by managers is to:

> ... communicate meaning and vision in symbolic ways which relate to the 'mundane' reality of those in the organisation. (Johnson, 1990)

This has been one of the problems facing quality assurance (discussed further in Chapter 9). Partners can present it in a visionary way, but very often trivial procedures have simply not made sense to those doing the day-to-day work.

Positive feedback is also crucial to the process. Again drawing from experience in QA, the Norwegian Building Research Institute (Sjoholt, 1989) specifically looks for solutions to problems the **firms** identify in order to create quick gains in the initial stages of implementation. In this way enthusiasm for the process can be generated within the firms. Once this has been achieved, a move is made on the overall system design.

(c) *Refreezing*

If people have been involved in the change process and feel ownership, it is quite possible that, at an individual level, the new norms and behaviour patterns will be internalized with no problems. At the organizational level there are two areas at which action can be taken to reinforce the changes: structure and technology.

In terms of **structure** the challenge is to move from a task force mentality to a 'business as usual' frame of mind. However the firm is structured, it should reflect the new mode of operating and the key personnel should be very carefully chosen to ensure that the momentum is maintained. Here the issue of 'sunk costs' can be used to advantage. People who have invested a lot of time and energy in a change process are hardly likely to allow it to wither.

The **technology** developed, such as procedures and sources of encoded knowledge, again should be carefully set up to reinforce rather than undermine the change.

Structure and technology are key areas in which the ecology of the firm can be designed to support and maintain the new social processes created by the change process.

8.5 ALTERNATIVE APPROACHES

8.5.1 Change v. stability

So far the forces for change and positive ways to react have been stressed, but is change a 'good thing'? Should it be accepted unquestioningly or treated with caution?

Some writers (e.g. Hurst, 1984) have argued that change is intrinsically good for organizations and have described firms that purposefully create turbulence in order to keep things fresh and dynamic. At the other extreme, it has already been indicated that it is quite normal for change to be resisted.

Louis and Sutton (1991) treat this issue in terms of how people think. They contrast 'active thinking' with 'habits of mind' and observe that the former are often thought to be better *per se*. In contrast they take a contingency approach and acknowledge that for much of the time, for 'business as usual', habits of mind are appropriate, whereas in conditions of novelty, discrepancy or for a deliberate initiative, **active thinking** is required. Their analysis focuses particularly on 'switching cognitive gears' between the two modes and they suggest various barriers to switching from the automatic to the conscious mode of thinking. For example:

- if the firm has rigid norms and values;
- if the firm has experienced extended periods of success;
- if the stimulus for change is minor or massive (not in between), 'threat-rigidity effects' can operate in latter case;
- if the required change is not incremental, but demands 'double loop learning' (Argyris and Schon, 1978).

The authors argue that individuals need to be adept at both modes of thinking and that possibly the most important thing is to '... improve one's capacity to read the situation ...' so that the need to change one's approach is recognized. There is a danger that just when an organization needs to change most it will be least able to.

8.5.2 Summary

It would be wrong to try to label 'change' good or bad. It is appropriate in some circumstances and simply a distraction in others. Thus, sensitivity is needed to identify when change is required and then to choose, or facilitate, the appropriate way to effect it, probably involving some combination of formal and informal mechanisms.

8.6 CONCLUSION

Professional firms involved in construction are facing unprecedented rates of change in their environment. This demands a reaction, but change within the firm is often resisted. Overcoming this resistance is greatly aided by viewing change as a process, not an event. Further, to achieve lasting change attention must be paid to preparing the ground and, afterwards, reinforcing the change.

Change within the professional firm is not good or bad *per se*, but in the turbulent environment currently faced it is likely to be appropriate. Given the conservative nature of the construction industry, concerted efforts are required to achieve changes successfully and formal and informal mechanisms should be used in a complementary way.

PART FOUR

Research perspective

Future issues

9

Various future trends have already been mentioned in the Introduction and in the last chapter in relation to the management of change. In this chapter two key aspects of the business environment for the construction professions will be dealt with in some detail.

First, 'quality management' will be considered and then aspects of client relations as illuminated by consideration of ways in which clients' briefs are changing.

9.1 QUALITY MANAGEMENT

9.1.1 Introduction

Over the last five years quality assurance has been one of the most prominent topics of discussion within the construction industry in general and surveying in particular. The issue has been fairly straightforward: either you become third party registered for quality assurance using BS 5750, (BSI, 1987) or you don't. Some firms have vigorously pursued this route, but many have expressed reservations and at best moved more slowly. CIRIA has found that some 40 out of an estimated 10 000 professional firms involved in construction have so far been entered on the DTI's register of Quality Assured firms. This represents a take up of 0.4% (CIRIA, 1990).

Of those firms that have become registered there is a preponderance of large firms, and it has been suggested that it would be impossible to register small firms with only one practitioner (who does the checking?) and some say that firms with only two or three practitioners could bring QA into disrepute (Murta, 1990). If this view is accepted then around 50% of the professional firms involved in construction are automatically excluded.

It is clear from many discussions that the motivating force for firms to strive for registration is rooted in marketing considerations. For some it is simply that they feel clients, at some stage in the future, will demand registration. For others it is a case of gaining a competitive edge. Strangely, and nobody seems particularly perturbed by this, very few people give as their primary reason a desire to achieve a consistent high-quality output.

So, in summary, quality assurance in the UK has become synonymous with, first, BS 5750, Parts 1–4 and, second, third party certification. Nevertheless, debate has been raging in academic circles, distinctly different approaches have been taken in other countries and there have recently been rapid developments in the relevant international and national standards.

The remainder of this section will deal in turn with the fundamental nature of quality management, the current position regarding standards and, lastly, the question of third party certification.

9.1.2 What is quality management?

Over the last few years an industry has grown up around quality assurance (QA), fuelled to an extent by the fairly generous grants available from the DTI for QA consultancy, but also necessitated by the uneasy fit between the available standards and the operations of those involved in the construction profession. As a result, QA has been seen as a separate subject upon which one has to be an expert to comment. This has tended to insulate QA from critical analysis due to its newness and the resultant dearth of experience to judge it by. It is only recently that it has become more generally accepted that QA is in fact **management**. This may seem a trivial point, but is in fact crucial to the development of the discipline. The moment the discussion is put in this context it becomes apparent that QA, as has been practised within the UK to date, is in fact a particular approach to managing the quality aspects of the operations of firms (Barrett, 1989). It is a small step from this statement to suggest that there may be other approaches and to draw on the voluminous management literature to assess the likely benefits of the available alternatives.

When the issue is viewed in this way, the term quality management (QM) will be used in preference to quality assurance (QA). As will be seen later, this encapsulates another important distinction.

It is easy to forget that construction professionals did **manage** their practices before the advent of QA, many continue to do so and, for a host of firms, high-quality output has been and still is achieved. In short, there are many highly experienced managers within the relevant professions who have long track records of successfully leading firms to produce high-quality work. The body of knowledge they represent is of immense importance, but has so far been largely ignored while the profession is dazzled in the headlights of the QA machine driven by the government and the consultants. As a result there has been the faintly ridiculous situation of experienced partners being told what they must do to run their practices effectively by people who may well not have had any previous experience in the construction professions.

One very important way forward is to infuse the development of QM as a subject by drawing from this wealth of experience.

Turning now to the management literature, it is fortuitous that over the last decade there has been a rapid growth in the study of the service sector of the economy, stimulated particularly by work in Scandinavia (Grönroos, 1984). Much space has been devoted to highlighting the fundamental differences between manufacturing and service businesses. The key dimensions of services that must be taken into account are the **intangibility** of services and the existence of buyer–seller **interactions**. In plain English this means that it is difficult to pick a service up, weigh it in your hand and look at it; furthermore, a service cannot be made in a factory or handed over to a marketing department to be packaged for the buyer. The professions are part of the service sector and the work they do involves complex interpersonal relations with their clients. These interactions have already been discussed in Chapter 4 are of key importance to achieving a high-quality service.

It has been suggested that client satisfaction will depend on the client making a judgement based on the **expectation** of the service to be provided and the **perception** of what actually results. This creates the expectation–perception gap already shown in Figure 4.5.

From that diagram it can be seen that **how** the service is provided as well as **what** is actually done are both important, and that the whole process depends to a great extent on personal opinions.

If it is accepted that these aspects accurately represent the essentials of the client's assessment of service quality, then they should be central to the QM systems used. It is probably fair to say that the standards used to date have not reflected these aspects, primarily because they were written for the manufacturing industry.

Figure 9.1 (Barrett, 1989) suggests circumstances in which the approach taken to date would appear to be **appropriate** and it can be seen that the influences show a tendency towards a production line type of situation. The **alternatives** given suggest other means by which consistent high-quality work could perhaps be achieved and are drawn from a strand of management literature in America (Kerr, 1977; Kerr and Slocum, 1981; Manz and Sims, 1987) that has been arguing for individuals to be given greater responsibility in order to achieve consistent high-quality work. The extent to which the suggestions mirror the traditional approach to work in the professions is very noticeable!

In summary, QM is **management**. To date the approach taken has been limited to one interpretation only. There are other alternatives and a major source of ideas must be the experience built up within the profession over the years. Drawing from the management literature, the client's perception of the service is of key importance and this introduces 'soft' aspects which do not sit easily with the standards used to date. The next section will consider recent developments in those standards.

9.1.3 Developments in the standards

Until 30 September 1991 firms that wanted to become involved in QA had only one standard to turn to, namely BS 5750, Parts 1–3. This was originally written for the manufacturing industry and, as a result, was difficult to use for construction in general and professional firms involved in construction in particular. As a result, a number of interpretive documents have been issued in recent years (Oliver, 1990; RIBAIR, 1989), all of which endeavour to translate the structure and wording of the standard to fit the customs and practice of the construction industry. For professional firms, titles like 'handling, storage, packaging and delivery' have never seemed immediately relevant!

Nevertheless firms that were determined to make progress in this area have made tremendous efforts and a number have become registered. While this was the only standard, any firm that wanted to pursue its commitment to QA could do little other than comply with it, particularly in the UK context. However, since 30 September 1991 a new standard has been available within the UK, namely BS 5750, Part 8. This is in fact an International Standard, ISO 9004-2 (ISO, 1990) around which the British Standards Institute has put a cover. The relevance of this standard is that it is written specifically for **services** and it lists professional services, including surveying and architecture, in Annex A, as examples of sectors to which the standard may properly be applied.

Initial press reaction to the standard described it as 'an interpretive document for BS 5750 Parts 1 to 3' (Anon., 1991). In the author's view, this is quite wrong. One would expect an interpretive document to correspond broadly with that which is being interpreted, whereas ISO 9004-2 is written in a completely different order (see Annex B of the standard for cross referencing). The reality is that this new standard is written specifically about internal QM systems for services as opposed to the original standards, which are rooted in the manufacturing industry. Given the major distinctions that need to be made between the two types of industry, already outlined above, one would anticipate quite considerable differences in the contents of the respective standards.

Even on a brief perusal of ISO 9004-2 it is evident that it is indeed quite different. For example, the introduction mentions human aspects, social processes, customers' perception, image, culture and motivation. Perhaps, most importantly,

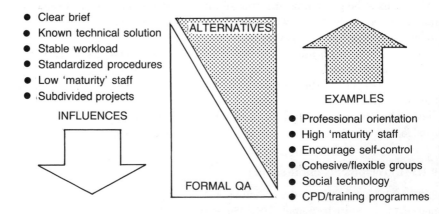

- Clear brief
- Known technical solution
- Stable workload
- Standardized procedures
- Low 'maturity' staff
- Subdivided projects

INFLUENCES

ALTERNATIVES

FORMAL QA

EXAMPLES

- Professional orientation
- High 'maturity' staff
- Encourage self-control
- Cohesive/flexible groups
- Social technology
- CPD/training programmes

Fig. 9.1 Factors supporting QA/alternatives

it stresses that 'customer assessment is the ultimate measure of the quality of the service' (Clause 6.3.3). In addition, it is stated that qualitative ('soft') as well as quantitative characteristics must be taken into account (Clause 4.1). Both of these aspects strongly reflect the influence of the service management literature mentioned above.

The coordinating diagram provided by the standard, which describes the 'service quality loop', is given in Figure 9.2.

In addition to the prominence given to the customer's assessment there is also a key 'box' shown in the diagram in which performance is analysed and **improved**. This effectively represents the organization learning (Argyris and Schon, 1978) and constantly improving its performance over time.

Before leaving the question of standards it is interesting to consider the definition of total quality management (TQM) given in the draft addendum of ISO 8402 (ISO, 1989):

> Item 3.50, total quality management: a way of managing an organisation which aims at the continuous participation and cooperation of all its members in the improvement of:
> – the quality of its products and services
>   the quality of its activities
> – the quality of its goals
> to achieve customer satisfaction, long-term profitability of the organisation and the benefit of its members, in accordance with the requirements of society.

Taking this and ISO 9004-2, it can be seen that a strong framework for the creation of QM systems within professional firms is now developing and that TQM provides the opportunity to extend consideration beyond the day-to-day provision of services by introducing many contextual issues.

Because the new standard reflects much more closely the familiar concerns of professional firms it should be much easier for them to develop systems based on their existing experience, and the TQM definition suggests that they should then link this with the aims of the organization and its members and the requirements of society. The objective becomes incremental, but continuous, improvements.

9.1.4 Third party certification

There are three ways in which QM systems can be checked, namely: third party certification, second party certification and first party certification. With first party certification the organization checks its own systems. In the case of second party certification, a client would check the systems of a firm he or she intended to use with a particular project or type of work in mind. Third party certification is where independent assessors, selected from a DTI list, visit the firm to check its systems, and if they are found to be acceptable the firm's compliance with the relevant standard is confirmed.

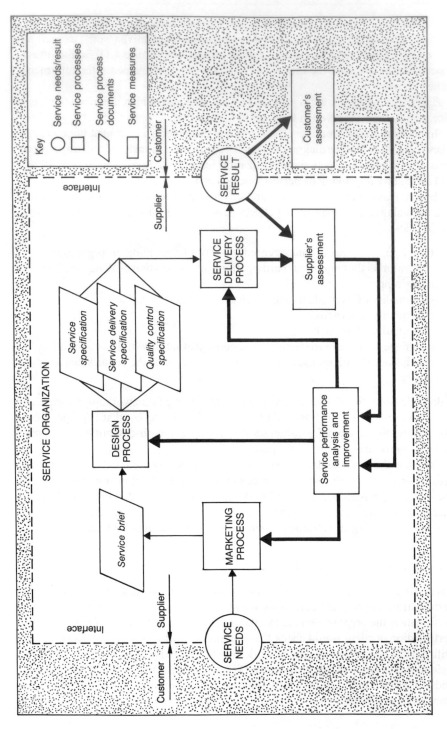

Fig. 9.2 Service quality loop

As stated at the start of this chapter, third party certification within the UK is often viewed as an intrinsic part of QA. This, in fact, is a peculiarly British approach, which is not generally subscribed to in the property and construction industries of other countries. Implicit in this situation is the crucial point that QA or QM can be actively and rigorously pursued without including third party certification.

This is not to say that third party certification does not have potential strengths, but it must be stressed that it is not the only possible approach. For instance, firms can concentrate their efforts on actually improving the quality of their work through QM systems without stressing the 'assurance' part of the quality movement. In this case firms and clients could still both benefit as the improvements achieved would be reflected in the output of the firm. If a firm chose this approach it would probably engage in some internal checking, and this might come into the category of first party certification.

Another alternative is second party certification, which could be done with particular clients and could, in fact, form part of the briefing process, with discussion leading to agreement between the client and the professional firm as to which procedures will be implemented for a particular project. This approach has the benefit of a tailored solution to suit a set of specific demands. The variable to consider is the extent to which the discussion impinges on the internal management matters of the firm as opposed to those actions which comprise part of the delivered service itself.

It can therefore be seen that third party certification is not the only possible approach, but it has been very prevalent in the UK. It has the advantage of involving independent, experienced people who can provide ideas and take an objective view of the operations of the firm. However, various drawbacks with this approach have been identified. For instance, based on work at the Norwegian Building Research Institute, Odd Sjoholt (1991) has listed the following possible negative effects.

- Certification focuses on **paper systems** to the detriment of an efficient system of organization, and on quality assurance to the detriment of quality management and quality managers.
- The acquisition of a certificate becomes an aim and not a result, and this aim can damage a positive effort to achieve real quality.
- The issuing of the certificates according to the ISO 9000 is demanding, detailed and lacks flexibility.
- Large companies can intentionally spend money on the production of a paper system just to achieve advantages in the market.

Other factors are mentioned but the above are the main considerations. The emphasis on paper systems is almost entirely driven by the need to demonstrate to third parties that certain procedures have been followed. The danger is that, as a result of aiming for certification, firms may be tempted to take on paper systems developed elsewhere and impose them on the firm in order to achieve the quality 'tick'.

In reality, to achieve real improvements in quality, everyone in the firm needs to be involved; the systems are best grown from the 'shop floor' upwards and integrated, and there must be efforts to continuously improve performance rather than just break through a particular threshold.

A major issue in relation to third party certification is that of **client demands** for QA. This appears to be fuelled by the feeling that a third party quality assured firm will, without doubt, produce work to a more consistent quality than a non-registered firm. In this context it is interesting to know that Dr Duran – a leading American in the field who has been instrumental in the development of quality awareness in Japan – is not convinced. His view, given in a fairly recent Swedish interview, is as follows:

> The current development in Europe has taken an unfortunate direction. There is no evidence that a company using the ISO-9000 standards, or certified according to these, is any better quality-wise than other companies.

This statement was made in 1989 before the new standard was produced, but from a leading figure in the quality debate it is a highly discordant view.

In summary, third party certification is one approach to checking QM systems, but there are several alternatives. As a particular approach it has some advantages, but also carries many potential drawbacks. At the heart of the certification issue is the question as to whether efforts to demonstrate sound QM procedures

- reflect the **actual** quality of the work done and/or
- possibly **distract** attention and effort from the pursuance of good quality work.

There remains the important point that, at present, third party certification is a peculiarly British approach. Firms that do not want to get involved in this aspect should take heart that better QM can still be positively pursued without it.

9.1.5 Summary

In order to bring the various strands of this section together, it can be said that the pursuance of consistent high-quality output is a **management** issue. As such, the wealth of relevant experience already within the professions can and should be drawn upon, together with the growing body of service management literature. This leads to an approach which stresses client satisfaction, the inclusion of quantitative and qualitative aspects and the importance of individual personalities, self-control and motivation.

Up to 30 September 1991 the standards available were manufacturing based and their application was, rightly or wrongly, inextricably tied to third party certification. Since this date ISO 9004-2 (BS 5750, Part 8) has been available and is written specifically for services, with particular mention of the construction professions. This standard is focused on internal QM and stresses many of the aspects raised by the service management literature. Total quality management is providing a broader context for initiatives in this area, and central to this aspect is achieving a fit between the client's needs, the firm's needs, its staff's needs and society's needs.

Third party certification has a role to play but is not an essential component of QM. It can have some damaging effects in practice, in particular an overemphasis on paper systems.

9.1.6 Conclusion

It seems certain that, with the publication of the new standard, the quality debate within the UK will take a new direction. Hopefully, in years to come, the present approach will be seen as a first step in the right direction, a phase of development in which QA became an important issue, a symbol of the desire to work to consistently high standards. This stage achieved, QM must now evolve into a richer, more powerful approach, the tools, techniques and ethos of which are grounded in the reality of the organizations using it. In this way it should become widely adopted by construction-related professional firms, rather than being a minority sport for 0.4% of them and a source of increasing anxiety for the rest.

In order to move forward it will be necessary to draw on the wealth of experience already within firms. This will have developed over the years quite independently of the QA initiative, but those firms that have invested time, money and reputations in going resolutely for third party certification have a special core of knowledge as a result of the new ground they have broken.

In the coming years it seems likely that the focus will shift more towards QM, with an emphasis on the effects of different procedures on the quality of the output of the firm and, in a complementary fashion, it seems likely that third party certification will become of less importance. It may be that these changes will require a proactive debate with the professions' clients, possibly at government level, in order to focus attention at what really matters, namely, the consistent achievement of high-quality work.

In parallel with these developments it is probable that QM systems for the work of a firm will be complemented by a global approach for quality within firms encapsulated by the definition, given in this section, of total quality management. In addition, it is likely that the time dimension to QM systems will be strengthened. As well as meeting clients' current needs, systems will have to be sufficiently sensitive and flexible to adapt to new demands and, beyond this, they should be so designed to support and facilitate the anticipation of future demands (Law and Cousins, 1991).

The developments sketched out above are focused on individual firms, but it must be acknowledged that, within the construction industry at least, a critical area that needs urgent attention is the meshing of the QM systems of individual firms around and within the **construction project** (Fletcher, 1990).

Many firms have felt that they had to either pursue certification to BS 5750 Parts 1–3 or stand back from the QA initiatives going on around them. In reality there are many alternative approaches and, in particular, there is nothing to stop an individual firm, however small, deciding to make an effort to improve its existing systems in ways that make sense to those in the firm, who **should** draw from their own experience, but may also find ISO 9002-4 a useful framework.

A key stage in the QM process is establishing the client's brief (see Figure 9.2) and the next section considers this aspect in more detail in an attempt to identify trends in the client relationship.

9.2 THE CLIENT'S BRIEF

9.2.1 Introduction

Establishing the client's brief is, of course, a critical step in any construction project. By this means the client's requirements are set down: time, quality and cost parameters are defined around the central issue of the physical artefact desired by the client. Although this sounds straightforward the process is, of course, complex and the result is uncertain. This section reviews the traditional approach to briefing and then moves on to more complex views that provide indications of ways in which the relationship between clients and their professional advisers are likely to develop in the future.

9.2.2 Traditional views

The Banwell Report (MPBW, 1964) stated strongly that clients:

> seldom spend enough time at the outset on making clear in their minds exactly what they want or the programme of events required in order to achieve their objective.

It recommended that greater effort should be made to establish the brief, and further criticized professional advisers for not emphasizing that this is 'time well spent'. It is clear from this that the ideal brief was seen as a well-defined input at the start of the construction project.

The way in which the client's brief links into the construction process is very clearly defined in the RIBA Plan of Work (RIBA, 1967). Here the brief is developed from Stage A (Inception) through to Stage D (Sketch Design) via feasibility studies and outline proposals. It is then stated that the 'brief should not be modified after this point' – that is, no change should occur as the scheme is designed in detail, production information prepared, or while the works are tendered or executed. At the **end** of the process Stage M allows for 'Feedback'. The Plan of Work was criticized in a study by the Tavistock Institute for the '**sequential finality**' (Tavistock, 1966, p. 45) implied by the step-by-step process. The need to adapt to the client's changing needs and to new information as it comes to light are both stressed (p. 47).

A further area of concern revolves around the oversimplified use of the term 'client', which is often, in reality, an organization with competing factions. Thus Tavistock use the term 'client system' and suggest that there is a need:

to be very much more aware and responsible in developing the brief through a more conscious understanding of the whole field of social forces they must work with. (p. 40)

One reaction to this problem is provided in the Wood Report (NEDO, 1975), which focused on public sector clients and suggested that:

(a) a senior officer of the user department should be appointed as the client's representative for each project to coordinate requirements;
(b) for large or complex developments, a project manager should be appointed to assume overall responsibility.

Thus, a mechanism to orchestrate the requirements within the client organization is proposed and the integrating role of the project manager is suggested, typically focused on the construction team. An erosion of the traditional 'linking pin' role of the architect is implicit in the above developments, and the need for clear communication between the principal parties is thereby made explicit.

The above reports generally put forward a view that the 'traditional' approach to construction in the UK requires a full brief at the start and that this should not be changed thereafter. A dissenting view is provided by the work of the Tavistock Institute. From whichever angle it is viewed, successful briefing relies critically on good communication.

9.2.3 Briefing as communication

Bejder (1991) insightfully suggests the application of the Johari Window concept to the briefing process. This assists in the analysis of the process of communication involved and highlights possible problem areas. The framework provided by the Johari Window (adapted to the subject analysis) is given in Figure 9.3.

From the diagram it is clear that there are four main situations to consider. The 'public' area represents the client communicating, without difficulty, the requirements to the professional advisers. The 'blind' area can be seen to be the needs of the client that are identified by the adviser through two-way discussion (**feedback**) even though the client cannot initially articulate these needs. The 'private' area relates to the information that the client does not **disclose**, whether purposefully or not. The 'unknown' area is not known to the adviser or the client, but through the twin processes of feedback and disclosure this last area can be revealed, at least in part.

If the brief is to represent the client's requirements accurately and fully then the importance of advisers encouraging clear disclosure and providing feedback information to the client is apparent. This argues for close and free-flowing discussion possibly over a considerable period. This need not of necessity be limited to the early stages of the project.

The communication process is much more complicated if the 'client' is in fact

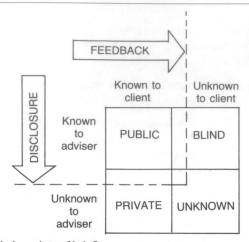

Fig. 9.3 Johari window view of briefing

a group of people or an organization. In this case the communications must be multi-stranded, both in terms of disclosure and feedback.

In the above, briefing is viewed in global terms. Recent work by Gameson (1991) has analysed, at a detailed level, the process of communication between clients and professionals in the initial stages of brief formation. This was achieved by recording the discussions and breaking down the content into categories. The predominant types of interaction were: 'giving orientation' (information) and 'giving opinions' with, to a lesser extent, 'agreeing'. Thus, **disclosure** and **feedback** are key areas as anticipated.

A very interesting finding was that the inputs from the parties varied considerably from one case to another, depending on the client's prior experience of construction. For instance, with an experienced client the architect only spoke for 36% of the time, while the client made a 64% input. In contrast, taking a case where the client had no previous experience of construction, the comparable percentages were 76% and 24%. A complete reversal.

It is clear from this work that the briefing process will be quite different depending on the level of experience of the client. This argues strongly for a **contingency approach** to briefing. The objective is to identify the appropriate approach to briefing in particular circumstances. One independent variable is clearly the project relevant knowledge-base of the client. Are there others?

9.2.4 Briefing as leadership

A fuller view of clients can be obtained by viewing the briefing situation in terms of the situational leadership theory introduced in Chapter 7. Here the distinction is made between the task-related needs of the follower and a sociometric dimension (Hersey and Blanchard, 1982).

Clients want their professional advisers to do something they cannot, or do not

	SUPPORT NEEDED	
	A LOT	VERY LITTLE
KNOWLEDGE NEEDED — A LOT	*'Help me through it'*	*'Give me the extra space'*
KNOWLEDGE NEEDED — VERY LITTLE	*'Do it so I can check it'*	*'Get on with it'*

Fig. 9.4 Typology of clients based on their needs

want to, do themselves. The relationship is founded on the adviser giving the client something the client lacks. In all commissions the client will expect the professional to 'get the job done', but the actual contribution made may differ considerably, especially at the early briefing stage, as shown in Gameson's work described above. This work did not, however, distinguish the two dimensions drawn from leadership theory. Taking these dimensions together a matrix can be formed, as shown in Figure 9.4.

The professional is generally leading, providing varying degrees of knowledge and support to the client depending on the client's particular needs. However, in the case of a very knowledgable, confident client, the roles may be reversed with the client taking the lead (influencing). The client types given in Figure 9.4 can be typified, as shown in Table 9.1.

Table 9.1 Suggested typical client types

Description	Explanation
'Help me ... '	Often the naive private individual involved in construction for the first and possibly only time in relation to a very personal project. A lot of knowledge and support required from the adviser.
'Do it ... '	This client is often a representative in a large organization which has a lot of its own procedures and requirements, for example many local authorities. The representative has to 'cover his back' and demands support for this despite a high level of relevant knowledge.
'Give me ... '	Clients in this category have little interest in construction *per se*. It is a means to an end, for example a factory extension required for increased production. Little support is needed, but a lot of knowledge must be supplied.
'Get on ... '	This client is knowledgeable and confident, say a developer client. He does not need support and can articulate his requirements clearly. That done, the onus is on the 'adviser'.

Although the above model is crude, the message is clear: advisers must diagnose their clients' individual needs if the appropriate input is to be provided to the briefing process.

9.2.5 Briefing as teamwork

The briefing process can be viewed as a **team** effort between the various parties. There are many categorizations of the various types of team members to be found in a team; however, to be effective such groupings should ideally have **complementary** abilities, and **compatible** underlying norms (e.g. Handy, 1985).

Based on his work in this area Powell (1991) argues that clients should:

understand their own needs first and then.. secure a design/build team who will reflect their own view of the world.

Clients should also choose a design team that displays a full range of **functional** roles and **team** roles by bringing together a group of complementary individuals, thus releasing latent synergy.

The functional skills have been discussed above in terms of the knowledge requirements of the project. At an individual level psychosocial factors have also been considered in terms of leadership. Powell's perspective extends consideration to include the group dynamics necessary for the team to achieve its objectives.

A central point in Powell's analysis is that:

the skills required to produce truly user responsive buildings can no longer exist in any one designer/builder.

Thus, the issue of effective groups is inescapable. This is very sweeping and, although undoubtedly resonant with a strong trend, it is possible to imagine a private individual with straightforward needs who would be manageable for a single designer.

The principal generator of the overload on the traditional designer is the need to accommodate a wide variety of perspectives within the client system if buildings are to be created that satisfy the wide range of demands. Thus, it can be seen that a fuller appreciation of the client's requirements leads to the need for a more elaborated construction team. And it is inevitable that the issues of communication and leadership discussed above will be of critical importance **within** the design team as well as between the client and the 'team'.

There is also the question of the contractor's early involvement, which seldom occurs in the traditional approach to construction in the UK. This has long been criticized and various newer approaches are allowing the beneficial inputs possible, such as Design and Build. This radically changes the roles of those involved in construction, and other forms such as Design Led and Build are emerging where architects are acting as lead consultants **and** contractors (Nicholson, 1991). There is not space here to pursue this area, but the issue is clear - the range of factors and involvement is variable on the building team side in just the same way as within the client system.

The above considerations are inextricably linked to the issue of a project management role drawing together the participants within the **construction system** and focusing them towards the client's objectives (e.g. Walker, 1984).

9.2.6. Views of the client

A key factor implicit in all steps of the discussion so far is that the starting point for any analysis should be the choice of view taken of the 'client' and the level of complexity thus admitted.

The Lancaster School of Management (e.g. Wilson, B, 1984) stresses the importance of the 'worldview' ('W' for *Weltanschuung*) taken of any problem that is being analysed. Solutions found will be inextricably bound up in the orientation of the decision maker. Ask an architect and you will get a design-biased answer; ask a quantity surveyor and you will get a financially-biased answer; ask an engineer and you will get a technology-biased answer; and so on. Over-simplified, yes, but broadly true.

Apply this to the question of briefing and it is clear that if an adviser's 'W' of his or her 'client' is of someone who has funds and is looking for a quick return, then the briefing process will be quite different in substance and style from an adviser whose 'W' includes, say, longer term issues, the user, and society at large.

Obviously the 'W' adopted will be conditioned by the client to a great extent, but there are many other forces at work such as education and professional conditioning and simply an awareness of the possibilities.

Drawing from his observation of trends in management consultancy, Garrett (1981) suggests that the consultant will often have to deal with the client and the 'problem-owner' (who is often not the client – for example, tenants), which has led to three different styles of consulting becoming evident. These are shown in Figure 9.5.

Expertise consulting is the traditional approach. **Process** consulting is where the consultant works predominantly with the problem-owner, but this can unsettle the client. Garrett favours **contingency** consulting, which is where the consultant draws out a solution from the client system, including both client and problem-

EXPERTISE	PROCESS	CONTINGENI
Client	Client	Client
Problem-owner Consultant	Problem-owner Consultant	Problem-owner Consultant

Fig. 9.5 Garrett's alternative consulting styles

owner. This assumes that '… most of the experiences needed to solve a client's problems are already in the organization.'

Research by Bejder (1991) in Denmark, which focused on university buildings, confirms the importance of involving in the briefing process all parties whose needs should ultimately be satisfied. In the study cited, the views of students, administrative staff, cleaners, maintenance workers, funders, designers and others were included. Comparing two building phases of the same university it was found that the appropriateness of the involvement in each phase correlated with the differences found in the quality of the buildings against a range of criteria.

This broadening of perspective when viewing the client system is consonant with recent developments in the field of facilities management (e.g. Becker, 1990, pp. 123–51) and with an increasing requirement from society in general and specific clients for their advisers to look well beyond the immediate building project and to take into account a whole range of environmental issues, such as healthy buildings and re-usable materials.

9.2.7 Summary

The question of the client's brief has been approached from a variety of directions. In mapping out the range of factors, and therefore actors, that should be involved, it has become clear that the formal, or traditional, view of the process is greatly over-simplified and excludes many factors that can be crucial. This coarsening of the analysis occurs both in the worldview ('W') taken of the client system and the 'W' of the building team. Generally, the architect and the particular part of the client system that has the need (the 'instigator') are the focus of the analysis. Figure 9.6 shows the parallel trends (Bertalanffy, 1971) within the two systems towards a broader view, symbolized by the **project manager** in the construction system and the **facilities manager** within the client system.

Taken together these trends suggest the development of a more holistic view which is bound to influence the briefing process.

When the project manager talks to the facility manager sparks should fly!

In addition to the range of factors involved, the **nature** of the interaction and the outcomes of different scenarios have also been considered. A **contingency approach** has been suggested, depending on the client's knowledge and confidence and also driven by the range of functional and team management skills required, which itself will depend on the breadth of view taken of the 'client'. Tentative evidence has been adduced to support the proposition that those whose needs you are trying to satisfy should be involved in the briefing process.

9.3 CONCLUSION

When those in construction approach the briefing process with a client it seems reasonable to suggest that they should initially consider:

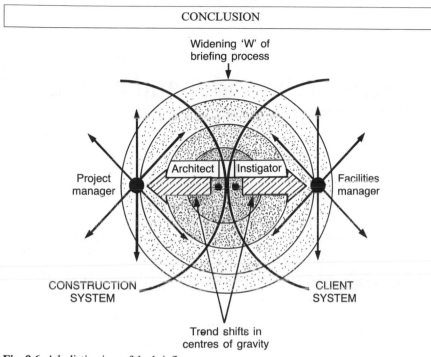

Fig. 9.6 A holistic view of the briefing process

(a) how extensive a view to take of the client and construction systems;
(b) the location of pertinent knowledge and experience – be it with the client, the
    designer, the contractor, etc ;
(c) contingent on the outcomes of (a) and (b), how to satisfy the client's needs
    through consideration of alternative structural and technological responses
    (Galbraith, 1973).

In any particular instance it is quite possible that the traditional approach will be
appropriate; however, it is also entirely conceivable that a broader view may be
required.

This is in good agreement with the discussion on quality management systems,
where it was suggested that the client's requirements should be given precedence
and the client's assessment taken as the major measure of the quality of the service
provided.

| 10 | Research model and results |

10.1 INTRODUCTION

This chapter describes a synthesis of management theory around the question: What are the main components of a professional service firm and how are they related? It is based on recent research (Barrett, 1989) focused on the construction-related professions.*

10.2 THE MAIN COMPONENTS

There are many models of organizations in the management literature. These are usually derived to suit the problem being analysed and so do not always include the same elements. To avoid unnecessarily limiting consideration from the start, a comprehensive model was sought.

The systems approach of Kast and Rosenzweig (1981) was chosen as a rough starting point, in terms of the major components to be considered. Their model includes the following and is similar, in whole or part, to many others (Leavitt, 1964; Kempner and Tregoe, 1965; Hersey and Blanchard, 1977, p.7):

- Environment
- Goals and values/psychosocial (people)
- Managerial
- Technical
- Structural

The above will be used as a starting point, but will be adapted as necessary as the discussion proceeds. The issue of how the parts are related will now be considered.

*Thanks are due to the Education Trust of the Royal Institute of Chartered Surveyors for financial support and to the professional firms that took part in the study.

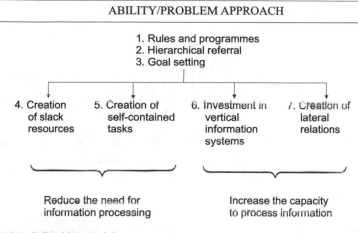

1. Rules and programmes
2. Hierarchical referral
3. Goal setting

4. Creation of slack resources

5. Creation of self-contained tasks

6. Investment in vertical information systems

7. Creation of lateral relations

Reduce the need for information processing

Increase the capacity to process information

Fig. 10.1 Galbraith's model

10.3 ABILITY/PROBLEM APPROACH

10.3.1 Information-processing view

Galbraith's (1973) information-processing view of organizations appears useful given the focus of this chapter on professional firms. These firms perform their function by applying their specialist knowledge for the benefit of their clients. This transfer of knowledge implies that information processing is at the heart of the professional firm. Galbraith's model is shown in Figure 10.1.

Galbraith's approach provides a common medium through which interactions within the organization can be viewed. The key variable in his analysis is the number of exceptions generated within the organization. When applied to professional firms the model is more realistic if all seven alternatives are treated as equally possible, rather than assuming that 1, 2 and 3 occur first due to the existence of a hierarchical framework. In reality the subject type of firm often has very little structure.

More fundamentally, Galbraith (1973, p.108) sees exceptions arising from the '… need to co-ordinate co-operative action'. That is, the analysis starts one step up the hierarchy focusing on coordinating individuals rather than considering what the individuals are actually doing. The characteristics of the people involved are not included as a variable. A standardized person is assumed. Given the patently variable nature of individuals this deficiency must be addressed.

So Galbraith's model gives a perspective that integrates the structural and technical aspects of the organization. The 'people' facet is not included. The importance of this facet can be crystallized by considering the extreme situation of a firm with very many highly competent staff (not unusual in the category of firms in question). (See Figure 10.2.)

It is suggested that a more fundamental measure for a firm is: the number of exceptions generated by the difference between the knowledge required to do the work and the knowledge actually possessed by those engaged on the tasks in

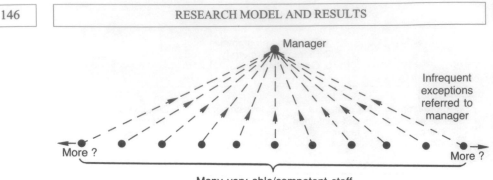

Fig. 10.2 Flat structure/competent staff

question. This accords with Sibson's view (1971, pp.152–3) that professionals at the lowest operating level must be the first focus of organizational analysis and thinking. This also shows resonance with the approaches of Hersey and Blanchard (1977, pp.157–8) who use 'maturity levels'; Herbst's (1976) 'competence ranges' and Maister, who considers this aspect specifically in relation to professional service firms (Maister, 1982).

10.3.2 A staff/project balance view

Maister treats the question of achieving fit between 'project types' and 'project team structures'. His typology of projects is similar to that of Woodward (1965), the extent to which the projects are similar to previous projects providing the basis of the categorization. Teams vary in their relative mix of junior and senior staff.

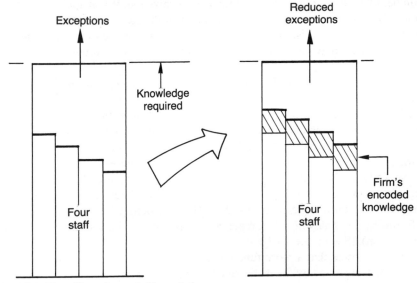

Fig. 10.3 The effect of encoded knowledge

Thus, where projects are repetitive firms can experience 'organizational learning' (Argyris and Schon, 1978) in terms of encoded procedures ('single-loop learning') or revised attitudes/approaches ('double-loop learning'). These are distinct from the individual learning of the members of the firm and comprise part of the technological base of the firm which is potentially available for the use of all staff.

The way in which technological support from the firm can reduce the generation of exceptions within the firm is shown in Figure 10.3. Four hypothetical members of staff are shown with varying degrees of knowledge, represented by the height of the bars.

Building on Maister's work the effects of different **structural** configurations are shown in Figure 10.4 (Barrett, 1987). Here the volume of exceptions is reduced by measures that either limit the difficulty of the tasks faced by the **individual** by facilitating specialization, or a structural form is used that allows people to work together, so helping each other out.

Galbraith's and Maister's models link well, but do tend to take the perspective of large organizations and thus possibly overemphasize formal variables. Maister's focus on firms ranging in size from 200 to 20 000 is certainly not typical for professional firms in the UK. For example, published statistics for structural engineers (IStructE, 1986) show that 89% of their members work for firms with 50 or fewer staff, 64% in firms ten or less strong and 22% as 'sole practitioners'.

This has implications for the categorization of members of the organizations as 'managers' or 'staff'. Only in exceptional circumstances are there any **full-time** managers. Kast and Rosenzweig's 'managerial subsystem' must therefore be interpreted in functional terms. People are managers when they manage. They are

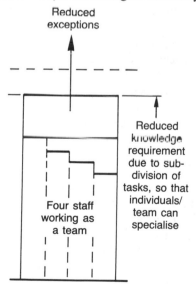

Fig. 10.4 The effects of structure on 'expectations'

staff when they are performing fee-earning work. Gummesson (1978, p.92) has specifically stressed the importance of this **part-time** mode of operating for professional firms.

The models discussed so far concern themselves with the processing of the organization's work: the projects. In some scenarios the management of the firm's future workload would be critical as junior staff with copious structural and technological support from the firm were 'fed' a particular type of work that they and the 'systems' could process. In this type of situation the firm must ensure that the right sort of work is delivered to the 'technical core' (Thompson, 1967).

The question of how the firm manages the future has yet to be confronted adequately. Planning the firm's future direction and translating this into reality by obtaining the desired workload, both in quantitative and qualitative terms, requires different skills and orientations which focus respectively on strategy and marketing.

10.3.3 A strategy/marketing view

Although strategic management and marketing are densely researched areas in the general management literature, it is only recently that there have been developments away from the mainstream theory specifically oriented towards service firms in general and, in some cases, specifically for professional firms. This new research emphasis appears to represent a lagged reaction to the changing composition of the economies of most developed countries, which have experienced a shift towards the service sector (Channon, 1978; Cowell, 1984). The 'Nordic School' has led the way with work by Gummesson (1978) and Grönroos (1984) whose work is complementary with further theories and research propounded by Wilson, A. (1984) in the UK.

A major factor stressed by the above is that with service firms 'production' and 'consumption' frequently occur simultaneously resulting in 'buyer-seller interactions' (Grönroos, 1984, p.36). For example, when an architect runs a site meeting at which the client is present, because the 'product' is in fact a service the client experiences both the production of the service and its consumption.

This factor is important because it results in the distinctive features of marketing and strategic management for service firms. First, the **whole** firm (or at least the visible majority) must be involved in marketing. This gives rise to the need for 'internal marketing' (Grönroos, 1984, pp.92–8), that is, actively managing staff to meet customer needs; to become 'customer-oriented'. Second, because of the highly specialist nature of professional services what is required is 'a professional who sells, not a professional salesperson' (Wittreich, 1969). Third, because a professional service firm is synonymous with the people that make it up to such an exaggerated degree, and because the management of staff–client interactions is so critical, marketing and strategic management are merely gradations on the time scale over which the firm is managed. They merge as the management perspective extends from one–two years up to five–ten years. So, there is the need for the firm

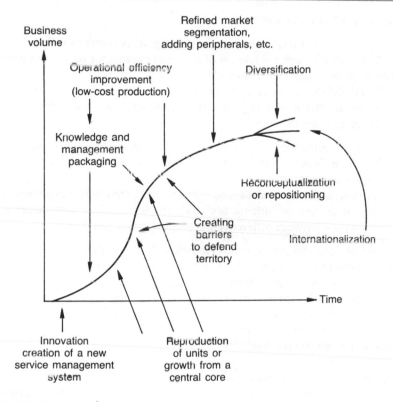

Fig. 10.5 The life cycle of a service

to effect 'a **continuous adaptation** of the operations to the customers' needs' (Grönroos, 1980). This requires a consideration of the management of the lifecycles of the firm's services (Foster, 1986; Webb, 1982). See Figure 10.5 for a typical representation (Sibson, 1971). Thus, both the marketing and strategic management in relation to the professional service firm concern the management of the firm **as a whole.**

As with Maister's and Galbraith's work the above ideas are focused on a limited span of organizational issues, principally the management of the firm's environment. Scant attention is given to many other factors, such as the effect of different worktypes for 'project team structures'.

A perspective that relates the various components and time frames is required. This can be achieved through what has been termed a 'process of argument' (Sidgewick, 1983). Rather than judging models valid or deficient, a formulation is sought that the given model holds true, but only within a certain ambit. The objective is to piece together the complementary parts of the models within the coordinating framework. To this end, the body of knowledge developed in cybernetics has something to offer.

10.3.4 A cybernetics view

Ashby stresses that one of the great advantages of cybernetics is that: 'It offers a single vocabulary and a single set of concepts suitable for representing the most diverse types of system' (Ashby, 1963).

Beer (1985) has taken cybernetics principles and applied them to **organizations** in particular. His model is *prima facie* complex, but in fact contributes two fundamentally simple ideas:

- An organization's environment is divided up depending on time scale, ranging from immediate to very long term, and the organization has to respond to the inputs from each zone.
- Each interaction between the organization and its environment will be in balance through the use of 'attenuators' and 'amplifiers'. The same applies to the interactions between different parts of the organization.

For the professional firm it seems reasonable to divide the business environment into current projects, current (and near future) environment and future environment. Using Beer's terminology: professionals working on projects is 'System One'; managers' supervision of this, 'System Three'; marketing and strategic management, 'System Four'; with 'System Five' providing the context (ethos) for the strategic thinking. Systems 'Two' and 'Three*' are specialist measures available for the internal management of the firm.

Despite the diversity depicted above, it is axiomatic to Beer's approach that each interaction is resolved (balanced) in the same way (Beer, 1985, p.27). This is by the use of 'attenuators' (e.g. summary management statistics) to communication channels that go from high variety sources to recipients of low variety, and 'amplifiers' (e.g. photocopied minutes) on channels going the other way. This is shown in Figure 10.6. Beer, like Galbraith, indicates that balance will pertain, if necessary at the expense of 'slack resources' (Galbraith, 1973, pp.15–16; Cyert and March, 1963), that is, suboptimal performance.

10.4 MODEL DEVELOPMENT

Drawing from the above views, the following summary description of the firm is suggested:

- It will distinguish between the firm and its environment and the various time scales (e.g. present and future) of the interactions between the two.
- It will show a flow of projects through the firm and a structure within the firm, comprising 'staff' and 'managers' designed to cope with the exceptions generated.
- It will have a place for 'organizational learning' of the firm and other measures that 'amplify' the abilities of staff/managers or 'attenuate' the difficulties they face.

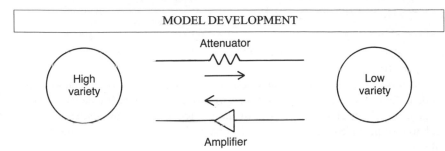

Fig. 10.6 Balance in information flows

Before describing the model diagrammatically various aspects will be considered to resolve the framework developed with Kast and Rosenzweig's model. This principally concerns the extra-individual aspects. Factors such as: 'encoded knowledge', 'computers', 'procedures', etc., appear fragmented, but Kast and Rosenzweig (1981, pp.109–11) call this collection of variables the **technical subsystem** of the firm. The above examples, and Beer's amplifiers and attenuators, can be subsumed into this single category, thus clarifying the model. This still leaves extra-individual aspects such as the groupings formed to do the work of the firm and the integrating measures used. These come within the **structural subsystem** of the firm. Having

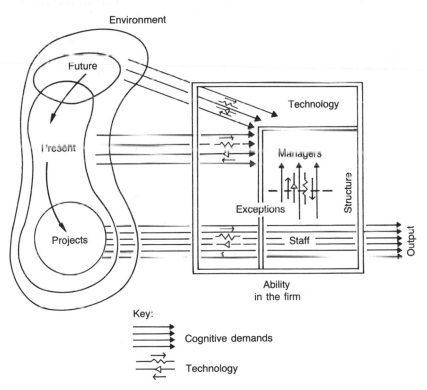

Fig. 10.7 Model of the firm – Stage I

developed the terminology to be used, the model of the firm reached so far is given in Figure 10.7.

The model shows the key interactions and at each link the same relationship is evident: tasks to be done of given levels of difficulty, people (managers or staff) of given levels of ability in respect of the particular tasks, supplemented by the technology provided by the firm and enhanced by supportive structural forms adopted.

10.4.1 Test of model—Stage I

To test the above model a sample of 36 professional firms was selected from the disciplines of architecture, building surveying, quantity surveying and structural engineering. Details of the firms and of their environments were collected via structured interviews and follow-up questionnaires.

In addition, some way of modelling the abilities of the staff of the firms was required. To this end a survey, by postal questionnaire, was carried out independently involving individual professionals of the subject professions. Six hundred and eight-four individuals responded and ability development was modelled using multiple regression analysis. This enabled the abilities of staff in the firms studied to be inputted

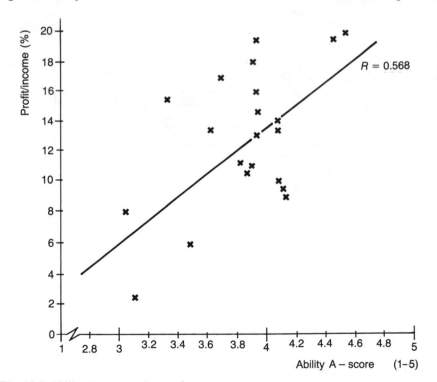

Fig. 10.8 Ability A-score against performance

via easy-to-obtain factual independent variables, such as number of years qualified. A full description of the fieldwork is given elsewhere (Barrett, 1989).

An **official goal** (Perrow, 1961) of high profitability was assumed and a ratio measurement of Profit/Income used to make comparison between firms' levels of performance possible. Each firm was assessed in terms of how **appropriately** it was organized and managed in respect of the key **ability-related** relationships identified in Figure 10.7. The resulting scattergram showing the correlation between 'appropriateness' (A-score) and performance is given in Figure 10.8. There is a clear correlation between the variables, but with a correlation coefficient (R) of 0.568 the A-score only allows prediction of 32.2% of the variation in performance.

10.5 THERE MUST BE MORE

Obviously the preceding model does not fully describe the situation. Referring back to Kast and Rosenzweig's model it is clear that it is the 'people' aspects that are barely represented. The model has been developed so far without drawing at all from the work of the behavioural sciences, social psychology, etc.

A link between the type of considerations reviewed so far and those now being discussed is provided by a commonly held (Kast and Rosenzweig, 1981, p.224; Shapero, 1985; Dawson, 1986) equation for the performance (P) of individuals:

$$P = f(a,m)$$
where a = ability
m = motivation.

That is, a person's performance is a function of his or her ability to do the work and his or her motivation.

Professional firms can rightly be termed 'people-intensive' organizations; thus it does not seem unreasonable to extend the above equation to the firm as a whole, with a and m becoming the summation of the values for the individuals. This links with the work of the Lancaster Systems Group. In the terminology developed by them an organization is a Human Activity System (HAS) and can be described by the following (Wilson, B., 1984):

$$HAS = \text{System of activities} + \text{Social system}$$

In this context it is clear that only the **ability-related** half of the issues have been modelled so far. What is now required is a model that captures the other, complementary, half: the **motivation-related** issues.

10.6 MOTIVATION/STIMULI MODEL

Given that the management literature relating to the motivation of humans is copious, well developed and, at the level used here, well known, it is not intended

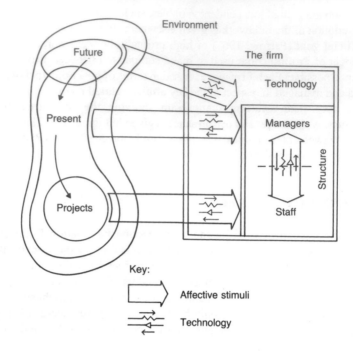

Fig. 10.9 Model of the firm – Stage II

to review it at any length. The main areas and principal sources drawn from are: individual motivation (Maslow, 1943; Herzberg, 1966; Porter and Lawler, 1968; Schein, 1972), work design (Hackman and Oldham, 1980), leadership (Hersey and Blanchard, 1977), and social psychology (Steiner, 1976; Brown, 1988; Wilke and Van Knippenberg 1988).

In each of the above areas theories have been propounded and normative advice given. As in the ability-related discussion it can be noted that almost invariably each specialist area has developed without regard to the issues treated in the other specialist areas. However, in some interesting work Kerr (1977) and Kerr and Slocum (1981) discusses the use of a wide variety of organizational devices as substitutes for formal leadership, with effective performance at the organization level as the overall choice criterion. He describes how characteristics of the subordinates themselves, the task and the organization in general can each exert an influence.

It is only a short step to consider all of the 'substitutes' and formal leadership to comprise a pool of **alternative** influences on the individuals in the firm. This view shows resonance with the schema commonly used in 'role theory' (Handy, 1985) with the individual subject to influences from his or her 'role set', i.e. all those who have some effect on the 'role-holder's' ultimate behaviour. The formulation here will, however, go beyond the interpersonal influences and include

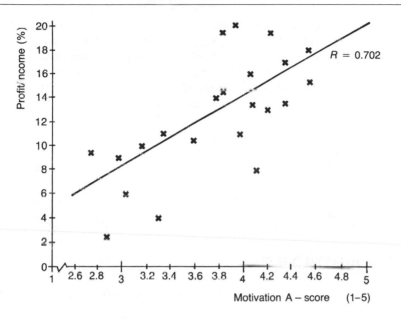

Fig. 10.10 Motivation A-score against performance

factors such as the characteristics of the tasks being done.

The model will therefore reflect the following features:

- It will address the individual's wants and sources of satisfaction, both current and future.
- It will consider the nature of the tasks being done and the motivational implications of their characteristics.
- It will include the manager/staff interaction as expressed in the leadership function.

As a framework for the description of the motivational issues the ability-centred model developed above will be used. It will be seen that at each interaction there are, in principle, the same components to consider: the needs of the focal person and the stimulus provided by the influencing factor. The suggested model is given in Figure 10.9. The model shows the 'managers' and 'staff' subject to different stimuli depending on the portion of the environment dealt with. It additionally shows the staff/manager relationship, with the managers able to choose how much of the firm's future to release to the staff through career progression.

10.6.1 Test of model—Stage II

As before the model was tested through fieldwork described in detail elsewhere (Barrett, 1989). This work included the subsidiary study of 684 individual professionals mentioned previously. At this stage findings of how abilities, motivations and attitudes varied among the sample were used to assess the **appropriateness** of the context provided by the firm to its members, in terms of motivation.

The scattergram given in Figure 10.10 shows the relationship found, within the sample of firms, between how appropriately they are organized and managed to elicit motivation, or effort, from managers/staff and their performance in terms of the profit/income ratio. In this instance the correlation coefficient is 0.702, that is 49% of the performance variation is explained by the motivation A-score. This is better than the predictive power of the ability A-score, but is still rather low. This is not surprising at this point in the discussion, because it is obvious that the factors which were central to the ability-centred analysis have not been included in the motivation-centred analysis.

The last section of this chapter will look at the effect of considering all of the factors together.

10.7 A HOLISTIC VIEW

Bertalanffy (1971), in describing 'General Systems Theory' (GST), illuminates two contradictory trends:

- that science is split into innumerable disciplines continually generating new subdisciplines ... and it is difficult to get a word from one cocoon to the other;
- independently of each other, similar problems and conceptions have evolved in widely different fields.

There is an identifiable parallelism between the models centred respectively on ability and motivational issues. In the first case the person is faced by tasks of given difficulty and what is at issue is how **capable** he or she is to do the work aided by the firm's technology and in the context of the structure of the firm. Thus, a **fit** between ability and task difficulty is at the centre of the analysis.

In the case of 'motivation' the amount of effort elicited depends on the fit between the needs/wants of the individual and the stimuli provided from various sources within the firm and in the firm's environment.

To weave the areas closely together a consistent terminology is desirable. From the work done on attitudes, it would appear that these are generally considered (Tull and Hawkins, 1976) to have three interrelated components: cognitive, affective and behavioural. Drawing from this, it would thus seem that individuals within the firm are subjected to **cognitive demands** and **affective stimuli** and the combined effects of these result in **behaviour** (performance). The integrated analytical model is given in Figure 10.11.

The main hypothesis of the study, related to that model, can now be stated as:

Within the context of the professional firm's environment, technology and structure, its performance is dependent on the extent to which a fit is achieved, for the individuals in the firm, in two areas:

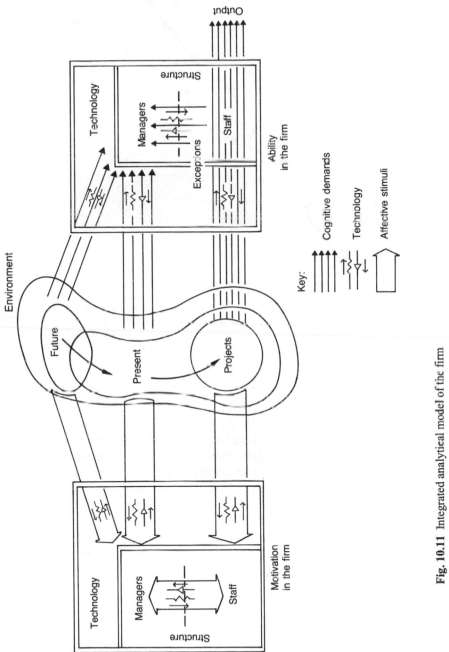

Fig. 10.11 Integrated analytical model of the firm

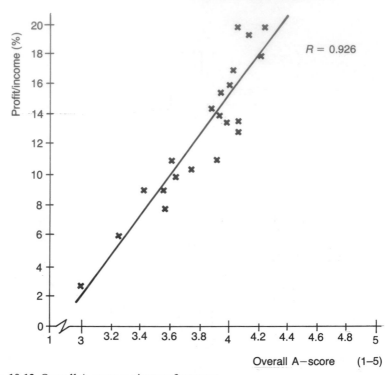

Fig. 10.12 Overall A-score against performance

- between abilities and cognitive demands
- between wants and affective stimuli.

All that remains is to consider how the combined effect of the two areas should be calculated. It was decided simply to add the ability and motivation A-scores with equal weight, after regression analysis confirmed that this gave the near-optimum correlation. Figure 10.12 shows the scatterplot of 'overall A-score' (calculated as described) and performance. The correlation is substantially better than either of the previous tests. With an R statistic of 0.926, 85.7% of the variation in performance is explained by the factors identified within the full analytical model. This is supportive of the $P = f(a, m)$ equation and the implication that the ability-centred model and the motivation-centred model are each **necessary**, but not **sufficient** to explain the differences in the performances of the firms.

10.8   CONCLUSION

The full model developed facilitates the explanation of the great majority of the variety of performance among the professional firms of the sample. It seems reasonable to conclude, therefore, that the model identifies the major organizational components and their relationships. The results support the inclusion of factors from both ability and motivation-focused theories and their combination with equal weight. Thus, the oft-stated but rarely tested equation $P = f(a, m)$ is supported by the results of this study. Additionally, the application of the equation at the aggregate organizational level proved successful.

It is hoped that others will find the framework of the full model useful in their studies as a description of the main components and interrelationships of the professional firm; and their implications for the performance of such a firm.

References

Adair, J. (1973) *Training for Communication*, Gower, London.

Anon (1991) Guide Prompts BSI Certification Doubts, *New Builder*, 10 October 1991, 10.

Argenti, J. (1980) *Practical Corporate Planning*, Allen and Unwin.

Argyris, C. (1962) *Interpersonal Competence and Organisational Effectiveness*, Tavistock Publications, London.

Argyris, C. and Schon, D. (1978) *Organisational Learning: A Theory of Action Perspective*, Addison Wesley.

Asch, S. (1955) Opinions and Social Pressures, *Scientific American*, November, 31–5.

Ashby, W. R. (1963) *Introduction to Cybernetics*, Wiley, New York, p.4.

Barrett, P. S. (1987) 'Co-ordinating framework', Practice Management for Chartered Buildings Surveyors, workshop, South Bank Polytechnic, London, 25 June.

Barrett, P. S. (1989) Practice management in selected construction-related professions, unpublished PhD thesis, CNAA, London.

Barrett, P. S. (1990a) *Practice Management and Performance in the Construction-related Professions*. Occasional Paper, Department of Surveying, University of Salford.

Barrett, P. S. (1990b) The Contingency Approach – A Positive View, *Graduate Management Research*, **5**, 3–10.

Barrett, P. S. (1991) Managing the Ability Gap for Structural Surveys, *Structural Survey*, **9**, 251–7.

Barrett, P. S. (1992) Managing the Ability Gap, in *Construction Management and Economics*, (eds R. Bon and W. Hughes), **10**, E. & F. N. Spon, London, p.40.

Barrett, P. S. and Hoxley, M. (1992) *The Synthesis of an Analytical Model of the Client–Professional Relationship*, Working Paper, University of Salford, Salford.

Barrett, P. S. and Males, A. R. (eds) (1991) *Practice Management: New Perspectives for the Construction Professional*, E. & F. N. Spon, London.

Barrett, P. S. and Ostergren, K. (1991) The Value of Keypersons in Professional Firms, in *Practice Management: New Perspectives for the Construction Professional*, (eds P. S. Barrett and A. R. Males, E. & F. N. Spon, London, pp.314–21.

Becker, F. (1990) *The Total Workplace: Facilities Management and the Elastic Organisation*, Van Nostrand Reinhold, New York.

Beer, S. (1985) *Diagnosing the System for Organisations*, Wiley, Chichester.

Bejder, E. (1991) From Client's Brief to End Use: The Pursuit of Quality, in *Practice Management: New Perspectives for the Construction Professional* (eds P.S. Barrett and A.R. Males), pp.193–203.

Belbin, R. M. (1981) *Management Teams: Why they Succeed or Fail*, Heinemann, London.

Bertalanffy, L. Von (1971) *General Systems Theory: Foundation, Development and Applications*, Allen Lane, The Penguin Press, p.29.

Bevelas, A. (1950) Communication Patterns in Task Orientated Groups, *Journal of the Acoustical Society of America*, 725–30.

Bierhoff, H. W. and Klein, R. (1988) Prosocial Behaviour, in *Introduction to Social Psychology*, (eds M. Hewstone *et al.*), Blackwell, Oxford.

Bono, E. de. (1971) *Lateral Thinking for Management*, McGraw-Hill, London.

Bonoma, T. V. (1982) Major Sales: Who Really Does the Buying? *Harvard Business Review*, May/June.

Brown, R. (1988) *Group Processes: Dynamics Within and Between Groups*, Blackwell, Oxford.

BSI (1987) *BS5750: Quality Systems*, British Standards Institute, London.

Burnstein, D., and F. Stasiowski (1982) *Project Management for the Design Professional*, The Architectural Press, London.

Canter, R. M. (1983) *The Change Masters: Corporate Entrepreneurs at Work*, George Allen and Unwin, London.

Carlisle, J. (1987) Strategy and Success in the Construction Industry, in *Managing Construction Worldwide*, (eds P. Lansley and P. Harlow) E. & F. N. Spon, London, pp.896–906.

Channon, D. F. (1978) *The Service Industries: Strategy, Structure and Financial Performance*, Macmillan, London.

Chaplin, C. R. (1989) *Creativity in Engineering Design: The Educational Function*, Report No FE 4, The Fellowship of Engineering, London.

Child, J. (1984) *Organisation: A Guide to Problems and Practice*, 2nd edition, Paul Chapman Publishing, London.

CIRIA (1990) CIRIA Launches New Project on Quality Management for Design, in *CIRIA Press Release*, London, January 1990.

Cowell, D. W. (1984) *The Marketing of Services*, Chap. 1, Heinemann, London.

Coxe, W. (1983) *Marketing Architectural and Engineering Services 2*, Van Nostrand Reinhold, New York

Coxe, W. *et al* (1987) *Success Strategies for the Design Professional*, McGraw-Hill, New York.

Cyert, R. M. and March, J. G. (1963) *A Behavioral Theory of the Firm*, Prentice-Hall, New Jersey.

Dadfar, H. and Gustavsson, P. (1989) *Organisation, Environment and Strategy Part 2: Strategy and Strategic Decision*, Working Paper 28, Umea University, Sweden.

Dalton, J. B. (1987) Quest for Quality, in *Managing Quality Worldwide*, 3 vols (eds. P. Lansley and P. Harlow), E. & F. N. Spon, London, pp.360–6.

Dawson, S. (1986) *Analysing Organisations*, Macmillan, Basingstoke, p.16.

Director General OFT (1986) *Restrictions on the Kind of Organisations Through Which Members of the Professions May Offer Their Services*, OFT, London.

Donnelly, J., Gibson, J. and Ivancevich, J. (1981) *Fundamentals of Management: Functions, Behaviour, Models*, Business Publications Inc, USA.

Etzioni, A. (1964) *Modern Organisations*, Prentice-Hall, New Jersey.

Etzioni, A. (1961) *A Comparative Analysis of Complex Organisations*, The Free Press, New York.

Festinger, L. (1957) *A Theory of Cognitive Dissonance*, Stanford University Press, Stanford, USA.

Fletcher, K. (1990) Key Elements for Quality Systems in Building Design and Building Contracting Firms, paper submitted to *CIB W-88 Meeting*, Oslo, 11 June 1990.

Foster, R. N. (1986) *Innovation: The Attacker's Advantage*, Macmillan, London.

Galbraith, J. R. (1973) *Designing Complex Organisations*, Addison-Wesley, Massachusetts, USA.

Gameson, R. (1991) Clients and Professionals: The Interface, in *Practice Management: New Perspectives for the Construction Professional* (eds P. S. Barrett and A. R. Males), E. & F. N. Spon, London.

Garrett, R. (1981) Facing Up to Change, in *Architects Journal*, 28/10/81 pp.838–42.

Getz, L. and Stasioski, F. (1984) *Financial Management for the Design Professional*.

Grönroos, C. (1980) Designing long range marketing strategy for services, *Long Range Planning*, **13**, 36–42.

Grönroos, C. (1984) *Strategic Management and Marketing in the Service Sector*, Chartwell-Bratt, Bromley.

Gummesson, E. (1978) Towards a theory of professional services marketing, *Industrial Marketing Management*, April, 89–95.

Hackman, J. R. and Oldham, G. R. (1976) Motivation Through the Design of Work: Test of a Theory, in *Organisational Behaviour and Human Performance*, August, pp.250–79.

Hackman, J. R. and Oldham, G. R. (1980) *Work Redesign*, Addison-Wesley, Massachusetts.

Handy, C.B. (1985) *Understanding Organizations*, Chapter 3, Penguin, Harmondsworth.

Head, G. O. and Head, J. D. (1988) *Managing, Marketing, and Budgeting for the A/E Office*, E. & F. N. Spon, London.

Herbst, P. G. (1976) Non-hierarchical organisations, in *Systems Thinking* (ed. Emery, F. E.), II, pp.245–58.

Hersey, P. and Blanchard, K. H. (1977) *Management of Organizational Behavior: Utilizing Human Resources*, Prentice-Hall, New Jersey.

Hersey, P. and Blanchard, K. H. (1982) ibid, 4th edition.

Hertzberg, F., Mausner, B., and Snyderman, B. (1959) *The Motivation to Work*, John Wiley, New York.

Herzberg, F. (1966) *Work and the Nature of Man*, The World Publishing Co.

Hurst, D. K. (1984) Of Boxes, Bubbles and Effective Management, *Harvard Business Review*, May–June, 78–88.

ISO (1989) *Draft Addendum 2, ISO 8402: Quality – Vocabulary*, International Organisation for Standardization, via British Standards Institution, London.

ISO (1990) *ISO 9004–2: Quality Management and Quality System Elements – Part 2: Guidelines for services*, International Organisation for Standardization, via British Standards Institution, London, as Part 8 of BS 5750.

IStructE, (1986) 'Development Plan' Working Party Report, *The Structural Engineer*, **64A**, 216–23.

Johnson, G. (1990) Managing Strategic Change: The Role of Symbolic Actions, *British Journal of Management*, **1**, 183–200.

Juran, J. N. (1989) Warning Against ISO 9000, in *Newsletter from the National Committee on Quality in Sweden*, No 4, Sweden, [in Swedish], quoted in Sjoholt, 1991, *op cit.*

Kast, F. E. and Rosenzweig, J. E. (1981) *Organization and Management: A Systems and Contingency Approach*, McGraw-Hill, p.19.

Katz, R. (1978) Job Longevity as a Situational Factor in Job Satisfaction, *Administrative Science Quarterly*, **23**, 204–23.

Kempner, C. H. and Tregoe, B. B. (1965) *The Rational Manager*, McGraw-Hill, pp. 191–2.

Kerr, S. (1977) Substitutes for Leadership: Some Implications for Organisational Design, *Organisational and Administrative Sciences*, **8**, 135–46.

Kerr, S. and J. W. Slocum (1981) Controlling the Performance of People in Organisations, in *Handbook of Organisational Design*, (eds P. C. Nystrom and W. H. Starbuck), Oxford University Press, UK.

Kindred, A. and Moreton, C. (1988) Managing Your Risk, presented at *The Members Conference*, RICS, 14/10/88, Birmingham.

Kolb, D. A. (1976) *The Learning Style Inventory Technical Manual*, MacBer, Boston.

Kotter, J. P. (1982) What Effective General Managers Really Do, in *Harvard Business Review*, Nov–Dec, pp.156–67.

Lansley, P. (1985) Putting Organisational Research into Perspective, *Construction Management and Economics*, **3**, 1–14.

Law, P. and Cousins, L. (1991) Is Quality Market-led?, in *Proceedings of the Fifth Annual Conference of the British Academy of Management*, University of Bath, 22–24 September, pp.15, 92.

Leavitt, H. J. (1964) Applied organisational change in industry: structural, technical and human approaches, in Cooper, W. W., Leavitt, H. J. and Shelley, M. W. (eds), *New Perspectives in Organisational Research*, **363**, pp.55–71.

Lewin, K. (1947) Frontiers in Group Dynamics, *Human Relations*, **I**, 5–41.

Lewis, P. (1991) Computerised Office Management for Professional Practices in Construction, in *Practice Management: New Perspectives for the Construction Professional*, (eds P. Barrett and A. R. Males) E. & F. N. Spon, London, pp.274–82.

Louis, M. R. and Sutton R. I. (1991) Switching Cognitive Gears: From Habits of Mind to Active Thinking, *Human Relations*, **44**, **(1)**.

MAC (1985) *Competition and the Chartered Surveyor: Changing Client Demand for the Chartered Surveyor*, RICS, London.

Maister, D. H. (1982) 'Balancing the professional service firm', *Sloan Management Review*, Fall, 15–29.

Maister, D. (1989) *Professional Service Firm Management*, 4th edition, Maister Associates Inc., Boston.

Manz, C. C. and H. P. Sims (1987) Leading Workers to Lead Themselves: The External Leadership of Self-managing Work Teams, *Administrative Science Quarterly*, **32**, 106–28.

Maslow, A. H. (1943) 'A theory of human performance', *Psychological Review*, July, 370–96.

McFadzean-Ferguson, P. R. (1985) *Changes in UK Civil Engineering Consulting 1974–84: Some Implications*. Unpublished MSc Disseration, Imperial College of Science and Technology, London.

McGee, J. (1985) Environmental Changes and the Internal Management of Building Surveyors' Partnerships: Strategy in Private Practice, presented at *Building Surveyors' Annual Symposium*, 31/10/85, RICS, London.

McGregor, D. M. (1957) The Human Side of Enterprise, in *Adventures in Thought and Action*, Proceedings of the 5th Anniversary Convocation of the School of Industrial Management, MIT, USA, pp.23–30.

Mintzberg, H. and Waters, J. A. (1985) Of Strategies Deliberate and Emergent, *Strategic Management Journal*, **6**, 257–72.

Moxley, R. (1984) *The Architects Guide to Fee Negotiations*, Architectural Press Ltd, London.

MPBW (1964) *The Placing and Management of Contracts for Building and Civil Engineering Work (Banwell Report)*, HMSO, London.

Murta, K. (1990) 'European Attitudes' paper presented to *CIB W 88 Meeting*, Oslo, 11 June 1990.

NEDO (1975) *The Public Client and the Construction Industries (Wood Report)*, HMSO, London.

Newman, W. H. (1975) *Constructive Control*, Prentice–Hall, New Jersey.

Nicholson, M. P. (1991) The Procurement of Architectural Design Services, Particularly Regarding Design and Build Contracts, in *Practice Management: New Perspectives for the Construction Professional* (eds P. S. Barrett and A. R. Males), E. & F. N. Spon, London, pp.50–8.

Nisbet, J. (1977) The Changing Nature of Professional Practice, in *Chartered Surveyor*, April, 285–9.

Oliver, B. (1990) *Quality Management in Construction: Interpretations of BS 5750 (1987) – 'Quality Systems' for the Construction Industry*, CIRIA Special Publication 74, London.

Perrin, S. and Spencer, C. (1981) Independence or Conformity in the Asch Experiment as a Reflection of Cultural and Situational Factors, *British Journal of Social Psychology*, **20**, 205–9.

Perrow, C. (1961) The analysis of goals in complex organizations, *American Sociological Review*, **26**, 855.

Porter, L. W. and Lawler, E. E. (1968) *Managerial Attitudes and Performance*, Irwin, Illinois.

Powell, J. A. (1991) Clients, designers and contractors: the harmony of able design teams, in *Practice Management: New Perspectives for the Construction Professional*, (eds P. S. Barrett and A. R. Males), E. & F. N. Spon, London, pp.137–48.

RIBA (1962) *The Architect and His Office*. RIBA, London.

RIBA (1967) *Plan of Work*, RIBA, London.

RIBAIR (1989) *Quality Assurance: Guidance on Assessment and Notes for Firms*, RIBAIR, London.

RICS (1988) New Rules of Conduct in Force, in *Chartered Surveyor Weekly*, 3–10/3/88, 67–68.

RICS (1991) *Market Requirements of the Profession*, RICS, London

Rueschemeyer, D. (1983) Professional Autonomy and the Social Control of Expertise, in *The Sociology of the Professions*, (eds R. Dingwall and P. Lewis) Macmillan, London, pp.38–58.

Rutte, C. G. and Wilke, H. A. M. (1985) Preference for Decision Structure in a Social Dilemma Situation, *European Journal of Social Psychology*, **15**, 367–70.

Schein, E.H. (1972) *Organizational Psychology*, 2nd edition, Prentice-Hall, New Jersey.

Schein, E. H. (1988) *Organizational Psychology*, 3rd edition, Prentice-Hall, New Jersey.

Schoderbek, C., Schoderbek, P. and Kefalas, A. (1980) *Management Systems: Conceptual Considerations*, Business Publications, Dallas, USA.

Shapero, A. (1985) *Managing Professional People: Understanding Creative Performance*, The Free Press, New York, p.62.

Sibson, R. E. (1971) *Managing Professional Services Enterprises: The Neglected Frontier*, Pitman, New York.

Sidgewick, A. (1893) *The Process of Argument: A Contribution to Logic*, Adam and Charles Black, London, pp. 32–3.

Sjoholt, O. (1989) The Norwegian Model for Establishing Quality Management, in *Building Enterprises, Building Research and Practice*, **5**, 289–93.

Sjoholt, O. (1991) Certification: A Disservice to Quality Assurance, in *Practice Management: New Perspectives for the Construction Professional*, (eds P. S. Barrett and A. R. Males), E. & F. N. Spon, London, pp.204–8.

Skinner, B. F. (1953) *Science and Human Behaviour*, MacMillan, New York.

Sherif, M. and Sherif, C. W. (1956) *An Outline of Social Psychology*, Harper and Row, New York.

Steiner, I. D. (1976) Task performing groups, in Thibaut, J. W. *et al.* (eds), *Contemporary Topics in Social Psychology*, General Learning Press, New Jersey, pp. 393–422.

Stogdill, R. M. and Coons, A. E. (eds) (1957) *Leader Behaviour, Its Description and Measurement*, Research Monograph No 88, Bureau of Business Research, The Ohio State University, USA.

Tavistock, (1966) *Interdependence and Uncertainty*, Tavistock Institute, London.

Thompson. J. D. (1967) *Organizations in Action*, McGraw-Hill, New York, p.21.

Tull, D. S. and Hawkins, D. I. (1976) *Marketing Research, Meaning, Method and Measurement*, Collier Macmillan, London.

Vroom, V. H. (1974) A New Look at Managerial Decision Making, *Organisational Dynamics*, **15**.

Walker, A. (1984) *Project Management in Construction*, Harper Collins, London.

Webb, S. G. (1982) *Marketing and Strategic Planning for Professional Service Firms*, Amacom, New York.

White, M. (1981) *Payment Systems in Britain*, Gower Press, London.

Wilke, H. and Van Knippenberg, A. (1988) 'Group performance', in *Introduction to Social Psychology*, (eds Hewstone, M. *et al.*), Blackwell, Oxford, pp. 315–49.

Wilson, A. (1984) *Practice Development for Professional Firms*, McGraw-Hill, London.

Wilson, B. (1984) *Systems: Concepts, Methodologies and Applications*, John Wiley, Chichester.

Wittreich, W. J. (1969) *Selling – A Prerequisite to Success as a Professional*, Wittreich Associates, Philadelphia p.10.

Woodward, J. (1965) *Industrial Organisation: Theory and Practice*, Oxford University Press, UK.

Index

Numbers given in *italic* refer to figures and numbers in **bold** to tables.